Below the Belt

Below the Belt

Sexuality, Religion and the American South

Angelia R. Wilson

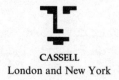

CASSELL
London and New York

Cassell

Wellington House, 125 Strand, London WC2R 0BB

370 Lexington Avenue, New York, NY 10017–6550

First published 2000

© Angelia R. Wilson 2000

British Library Cataloguing in Publication Data
A catalogue record for this book is available from the British
Library.
ISBN 0–304–33549–5 (hardback)
    0–304–33550–9 (paperback)

Library of Congress Cataloging-in-Publication Data
Wilson, Angelia R.
    Below the belt: sexuality, religion & the American South/
  Angelia R. Wilson
        p. cm.
    Includes bibliographical references and index.
    ISBN 0-304-33549-5 (hb.). – ISBN 0-304-33550-9 (pb.)
    1. Homosexuality–Southern States.   2. Southern States–
  Religious life and customs.   I. Title.
  HQ76.3.U52S678   1999
  306.76′6′0975–dc21   99-37830
                                                                        CIP

Typeset by Paston PrePress Ltd, Beccles, Suffolk
Printed and bound in Great Britain by Biddles Ltd,
Guildford and King's Lynn

*For my parents, Bill and Dorothy
and my siblings, Troy, Jack and Ginger*

ACKNOWLEDGEMENTS

"It takes a village." The entire process of writing *Below the Belt* involved various groups of people for whom my gratitude is endless: the friendly Southern folks who visited with this traveling stranger; the Faculty of Economic and Social Studies of the University of Manchester who supported the research with a Hayter-Perry grant; my late colleague Valerie Karn who found a bit more through her ingenious financing; Rebecca Dobash and Russell Dobash for their American-style encouragement; Joan Tronto, Anna Oakes, Jane Duckett, and Kath Dimmelow for commenting on rough drafts; and, of course, Janet Joyce and Dominic Shryane at Cassell who expertly guided the manuscript through the press.

This journey *Below the Belt* would have been so much more scary, and taken longer, without Sarah Dimmelow, my partner and best friend.

CONTENTS

Chapter One

WHAT THE HELL ARE YOU DOING?

Texan. Small-town Bible Belt preacher's daughter. Lesbian. Doctorate in political philosophy. University lecturer in England. That's pretty much me. I remember early one Sunday morning of a family vacation, we stopped at a little Baptist church just off a dirt road, somewhere in Mississippi. After church, when the locals realized we weren't kinfolk, one old man looked at my dad and asked, "But how did you get *here?*" My father, faithfully assuming that every backroad led to a main highway, realized the importance of that question when, just a few miles down the road, we came to a dead-end. I think of that story each time a Brit, noting the amount of sunshine in Texas, asks me why I live *here*. Well, I may not be at a dead-end, but turning 30 certainly caused me to pause and think about exactly how I got here. Given the categories of my identity listed above, it is not surprising that my ponderings resulted in a book about sexuality and religion.[1]

Once in Sunday School a male classmate asked what the scripture meant by "Adam knew Eve." Stuttering, the teacher explained that to know someone biblically referred to a husband "knowing" his wife on their wedding night. "Oh," replied the boy, "it means they had sex." We all giggled at the thought of sex being in the Bible. From then on, our pubescent minds equated the words "to know" with "to have sex." Later we were taught Biblical regulations about when sex was, and was not, appropriate and with whom. Church youth leaders were keen that we did not get to *know* one another. They instructed us girls on Christian dating with helpful hints, like "don't let him touch you below the shoulders or above the knees." Before marriage, we were responsible for making sure boys' "nature" did not get out of hand. I recall one lesson on the sins of masturbation in which "nature" was also not to be taken in hand.

As a young adult attending a small church-related college,

1

campus ministers told another bit of the story as they began preparing us for marriage. Ephesians 5:22–23 set out the basic guideline: "Wives, be subject to your husbands, as to the Lord. For the husband is the head of the wife as Christ is the head of the church, his body and is himself its Savior." Reader, you will come across this passage more than once here, but I guarantee you not as many times as I have heard it from the pulpit, counseling sessions, and boyfriends. In this lesson, we learned that because of their physical differences male and female had different roles to play in marriage, in the church, and in society. We learned that the Bible not only spoke of the sex act, it also regulated on the basis of sexual anatomy. And that "good" Christian men and women adhered to these God-given roles. I also learned that interpretation of scripture is powerful, and therefore dangerous. I try to avoid it here, although I do recall the uncomfortableness of others' interpretations.

In his rehearsal of the various interpretations of 'sexuality', Joseph Bristow notes the difficulty in locating an adequate definition: "Sexuality is surely connected with sex ... [but] ... the word sex is certainly ambiguous ... [it] refers not only to sexual activity (*to have sex*), it also marks the distinction between male and female anatomy (*to have a sex*)."[2] Under this umbrella, I would also locate social regulations which define appropriate sex acts and appropriate gender roles based on sexual anatomy. For example, many assume that because of physical differences men and women "naturally" should have different social roles. Such gendered roles based on physical, or perhaps even "natural" psychological differences proliferate in all western societies.[3] Southern girls, like their British sisters, are told how to look, act, dress, care, work, etc. in order to be proper, socially acceptable, women. Every girl and boy learns gender roles through social interaction and/or cultural osmosis. While these vary slightly between cultures, every western capitalist country builds Christian values into its political, economic, and social structure. And such values about sexuality, in turn, affect each of our lives, either directly through policies regulating marriage and the family, or more indirectly through cultural expectations of behavior.

Revisiting the lessons of sexuality taught to me has enabled me to understand a bit more about why, pardon the phrase, I am what I am. In addition, it has helped me understand more about the intersection of sexuality and religion in my homeland. The proliferation of conservative Christian morality distinguishes the South as the Bible Belt.[4] Combine that with the legacy of Southern genteel society and the resulting social atmosphere becomes imbued with gender, and sexual, clarity – Southern boys know what it means to be a man, and Southern girls know what it means to be a lady. It is as "natural" as the air they breathe. So here the first two chapters aspire to give the reader a whiff of this gendered, genteel Southern breeze.

Of course literature often describes the hot, humid Southern climate which evokes reckless passion both exhilarating and suffocating. Overwhelmed characters venture into improper sexual activity. In such a haze, clarity evaporates. So each chapter also gives voice to those who live and breathe in this Southern climate of gender/sexual complexity. In doing so, these chapters force a dialogue between those who embrace clarity and those who find it stifling. For example, second-wave feminism and the sexual revolution enabled women to claim their civil and sexual rights, empowering them as independent citizens and freeing sexual expression. Such empowerment caused all sorts of upsets to Southern sexual, and moral, certainty.

Perhaps then it comes as little surprise that one of the most fervent sexual–religious battles in American history was sparked off in the South. The Supreme Court decision in *Roe* v. *Wade*, allowing a woman to choose to have an abortion in the first three months of pregnancy, began in Texas when a single working-class white woman who did not want to have her baby asked a lawyer named Sarah Weddington for help.[5] Chapter 4 looks afresh at this debate through the eyes of Sarah Weddington and Flip Benham, director of the anti-abortion campaign group Operation Rescue. Interviews with each of them, as well as reflecting upon individual lives affected by *Roe* v. *Wade*, offers an insight into the labyrinthine world of what it means to choose life.

Chapter 5 builds on this theme of sexual–religious complexity. If the Christian Right has lost the legal war over abortion, they have certainly turned their network of moral artillery towards what they perceive to be the most significant battle in a contemporary moral war: rights granted to homosexuals. Constructed as behavior rather than identity, homosexuality is sin, and homosexuals are the devil incarnate. This religious positioning complements Southern gender norms and Confederate militancy, constituting the Bible Belt as no less than a living hell for gay men and lesbians – and the message of the Bible as nothing more than hatred. Noting the gap between this message and one of God's unconditional love, Christian gay men and lesbians are building churches based on diversity. These churches offer a spiritual home for gay and lesbian children of the South, who remain committed to the religious values inherent in their society. So while this chapter considers the effects of an agenda of hate, it also tells the stories of those who search for a new path through the sexual–religious maze. My final thoughts, found in Chapter 6, locate these stories broadly within academic literature as well as pose questions about future lessons of sexuality.

I LOVE TO TELL THE STORY

As a small child, I was given a collection of children's tales which my parents referred to as my "storybook." I was fascinated by the kings and princesses, the evil sorceress and helpful elves. As an adult, *Below the Belt* has become my "storybook." Unfortunately, it is not a fairy tale. Nevertheless, I find personal narratives of real lives equally as fascinating. The chapters here are filled with true stories – oral histories documenting contemporary life in the American South. They are stories from my homeland. Late one summer I embarked on a journey down the back roads of the Bible Belt – geographically somewhere just east of Atlanta, Georgia and stretching all the way to Abilene, Texas where there are more churches than traffic lights. In *The Lost Continent*, Bill Bryson travels across America in search of the small-town idyll of his youth.[6] Nostalgic Bryson was on a journey of discovery and was disappointed with what he found. Unlike Bryson, I was on a journey of hope. I hoped it would be different from when I left it.

So while during the writing process, I described my task as somewhat Brysonesque, it is a journey through Southern culture rather than a more conventional traveler's guide. Because, unlike Bryson, I actually got out of my car and chatted with folk. I am a good "visitor." "To visit" in the South is not just to pass through as a tourist. "Goin' visitin'" is to drop by a neighbor's, have a cup of coffee, and chat about whatever topic arises. Ever since I can remember, my father would take me visitin' with him. I sat for hours in the company of grown ups listening to stories of their daily activities; their childhoods; their pains and joys. So this book is simply an account of my visitin' with people across the South – a retelling of their stories, a collection of contemporary oral histories. Of course, just because I was fishing in my favorite spot didn't ensure they would be biting. When a stranger enters a small town and starts asking questions, they will get two types of answers: a glossy version bathing the town, or its people, in the best possible light, or a more colorful version painted by a local "character" who is either pulling your leg or enjoying his/her 15 minutes of fame. Strangers are not trusted with the truth. There are ways of overcoming this: being kin to someone in the town, which makes you one of them; having a local accent, which signifies a more general kinship of mind or values; or being able to sift through the civic pride and local characters to find the right people and to ask the right questions.

This is not the most scientific of methodologies. Even with my Southern accent, in the retelling of others' stories, I am forced to use my own voice. In my travels, in the visitin' and in the retelling, memories have been stirred. Sometimes they have brought a comfort, a settledness, a pride in who I am and where I am from. Sometimes they have rekindled pain or have reminded me to be angry or hurt. So amongst the stories here, is my story – my reflections on Southern culture and on my life in it. Needless to say, for all the above reasons, *Below the Belt* has been a fun, engaging, and difficult book to write.

HOME TRUTHS

Maybe part of that difficulty is a result of the various hats we adults wear, and the multiple expectations that accessorize them. As an academic, I wanted to hear stories about folks' values and then to locate those in relation to Confederate history and to the pervasive Christian morality definitive of the Bible Belt. As a native, and a small-town girl, I knew that the clearest picture of this relationship would be found in rural areas. Cities in general, but particularly in Southern America, are meccas of difference and alternative life-styles. City folk are, quite frankly, a bit more used to engaging with different types of people. Southern cities attract all kinds of weird folk, even Yankees. They also harbor sexual fugitives from rural morality. As a researcher, my mission could easily be scuppered by looking in the wrong place; accidentally speaking to someone who, dazzled by the bright lights of the big city, had morally swayed. If you're fishing for plain old bass, you don't go to an exotic pond, you go down to the creek. So it was to the less diverse rural South that I went in search of "Home Truths."

As a lecturer, I teach a course on social values and on the way in which public policies do or do not reflect those values. One of the theorists we consider is John Rawls. In his seminal text, *A Theory of Justice*, he argues that at the core of each human being resides a notion of justice.[7] If we could access that core definition of justice, then we could agree upon policies establishing a just society. In this intellectual exercise he outlines an imaginary situation in which that could be accomplished. Basically, his idea is that it is our differences that set us at odds with one other and in turn cloud our core sense of justice. So in this hypothetical space, we would rid ourselves of differences, enabling us to establish a just society. Although grossly over-generalized, that's Rawls' book in a nutshell. Now of course other theorists have argued that because his intellectual experiment can only ever be hypothetical – we can never rid ourselves of our differences – it does not help us implement justice in the real world. Others, Iris Marion Young for example, have argued that it is not in ridding ourselves of difference – all becoming the same – that we can know justice.[8] Instead it is in struggling with our differences that we define, or negotiate, justice. For Young the perfect example of different people living together harmoniously is the modern city – the common home of difference. Now in my opinion, that is a rather romantic view of a city. Frankly, the city ain't always a harmonious place to live; different people often get unjustly ghettoized in different sections of town. Nevertheless, it highlights one reason for avoiding the city. I wanted a Rawlsian kind of place where difference was minimized. For it is in a space where sameness is fairly certain and values are relatively clear, that one can begin to see the cost of difference. In the rural Bible Belt, gender/sexual complexity exacts a high price.

In the South there are worse things one can be than a lesbian: a Yankee, a communist, a feminist, a Black person. A lesbian, i.e., one who sleeps with women, "just ain't found the right man yet." So she is not seen as an immediate threat to Southern white male capitalist power. The South has always been a poor relative to the prosperous Yankees of the East Coast. Even in Texas, black gold doesn't buy the education or worldly sophistication associated with the North. Rural America is disappearing as capitalism's techno-logical revolution has moved jobs into the city. In the South, the shift toward technology and the service industry has left those remaining on the farm amongst America's most poor. In doing so it has left men without the economic means to fulfill their role as family provider. In addition, feminism has challenged their natural, if not divine, right as head of the household. By asserting their right to equality, women have taken power away from men in the home, workplace, and larger society. For some on the political far Right the first battle for men to retain their power must be fought, and won, in the home. For some on the (farther?) Right, the battle should be waged against others who have challenged their white supremacy – southern African-Americans. So while blame is laid upon the sexual and racial "other," the progressiveness of capital-ism[9] or the necessity of patriarchy[10] is never questioned.

Those who do not question capitalism or patriarchy, male privilege, are not unique to the American South. However, given

7

the history of slavery, where Black people became consumer goods purchased to make white life more convenient, the South is certainly a stronghold of capitalism. Additionally, given the history of Southern society, where (white) ladies were "protected" from education and work, and placed on a pedestal to be admired and possessed while (white) men maintained economic and political power, the South prides itself as a bastion of patriarchy. Finally, throw into this mixture a large dose of Southern Christianity. God, himself, sanctioned male dominance and female submission. Ask any preacher in the Bible Belt. Of course, there are Southerners that don't agree with these gender/sexual values – my ma and pa for example. But theirs and similar voices in this collection become the exceptions that prove the pervasiveness of the moral rules.

As noted above, most of these stories came from visits with Southern rural folk. While my "visitin'" methodology was not completely random – I organized a few interviews before the journey and utilized a substantial network of religious and professional contacts – it was nevertheless relatively open-ended. I got in a car and drove down the road. I stopped in 40 or so small towns – at Dairy Queens, Wal-Marts, grocery stores, bars, churches, and the odd adult bookstore. I struck up conversations over pecan pies, beers, lawn mowers, altar rails, and sex toys. A friend of my dad once said I was as shy as a bumble-bee. For the most part, I spoke with a damn good cross-section of people. With a couple of exceptions. Firstly, even for a well-trained dyke spotter like myself, it was pretty difficult to find "sexual deviants" in the small-town South. I know they are there. Hell, I was there half my life. But I also know that their closets are like Fort Knox. So a few of the interviews in the final chapters are with city folk. Folk who left their hometown to find acceptance, or anonymity, in the urban landscape. Secondly, few non-white, African-American or Latino voices tell their stories here. Undoubtedly the most problematic aspect of my methodology was my inability to build the necessary level of trust as a white stranger. The only interviews with Black people are those where common ground had been established beforehand, either through religious or gay and lesbian friends. My regret is only surpassed by my certainty that the white South will not own its racism until more African-American and Latino voices, more individual stories, are heard.

SKINNY DIPPING

Objectivity in the social sciences is a myth. It may be vaguely possible in the scientific empiricism of reporting how many of the population fall below the poverty line or how many married heterosexuals have 2.4 children. But even number crunchers admit that the statistics represent a matrix of social phenomena. The social world is far too complicated. Wait around for a bit and society, like the weather in Texas, will change. Surveys can give us a Kodak moment of society; they reflect a still-life pose of, or possibly a cinematic insight into, a particular scene. However, they tell us nothing of the effect of taking the picture: why were people posing in such a way? How did the perspective of the photographer determine the scene? The endeavor of research involves some sort of relationship, and interpretation, between the researcher and the subject. In short, I make no claims to objectivity. I have attempted to retell the stories here honestly and with respect to the people who were kind enough to sit and visit with me. Hell, even if it was possible, I couldn't write about my home without also writing about me: about how much I love it, and hate it; how much love I have experienced there, and my acute awareness that love is sometimes conditional; how much it taught me about life, and how much I learned only after I left it behind.

Because of my own relationship with the research, my nakedness as a writer, this has been the most difficult writing I have ever done. Primarily, my fear which has caused most pauses for reflection has been the importance of the task before me. How does one give a public voice to someone else's very private story? How do I tell, in their exact words, in the exact context, someone else's version of events, of truth? I certainly do not profess to have completed that task adequately. In order to provide coherence, I have had to produce another story, a meta-narrative that links characters who

9

do not sit easily together. In doing so, I have evoked my own voice, my own story. It is not one told from an ivory tower, nor is it one told as a researcher. Instead it is blatantly reflective of my own situatedness. So perhaps I should begin with my story.

I have always had this notion that I am different. But I am not. Zillions of people come from weird cultures with strange values that seem perfectly normal to them. Even if those values are not embraced, or even articulated. I am aware, Sigmund, that this notion of difference has probably arisen from my childhood. During the first 20 years of my life I lived in eight different small towns across the Panhandle of Texas. Significantly, my four years in high school were spent in three different towns, each with a population of less than a thousand. For that reason alone, moving from small, tightknit town to small, tightknit town in those first years of puberty, I was always different. Like *Pleasantville*, no one ever moved away, no one ever moved in. Except for the teacher's families, and the preacher's families. I was part of the latter. Our family was different, outsiders.

But then again, we were like most white working-class Southerners. My mother is an amazing woman, whose mother died when my mom was just ten years old, leaving her to raise four younger sisters. My grandfather was a share-cropper, meaning poverty was a way of life. In 1968 at 33 years of age, after raising her sisters, and having four children of her own, my mother decided to become a nurse. With nothing more than a tenth-grade education herself, three kids in high school and one in kindergarten, and working a full-time night job, college was a brave, if not slightly crazy, step. She wasn't aware of second-wave feminism, she *was* it. Her life has influenced me beyond the place that my words can now take me. No doubt you will find her in this book, but it is most likely my father's occupation, his position, his beliefs that continue to influence me. Unlike Church of England vicars, or the large majority of Protestant ministers in the South, my father is not middle class. As the youngest of six children in a small cotton town, he began his working life following in his father's footsteps pumping gas. When he married my mother – she was 16, he was 17 – they lived with his parents in a stone house my grandfather and uncles had built before the Second World War. My father has recently retired and has bought that very house. It is the first house he and mother have ever lived in that they have owned. At 30 years of age, with three children, he felt the call to the ministry. With a ninth-grade education, he began two years of college training to become a Methodist preacher. I was born at his first parish. Of course I don't remember it, but I do remember the third. Hedley, Texas has less than four hundred people, and at the time, four churches. The six of us lived in a two-bedroom parsonage, my brothers slept on the enclosed porch. It was the only time I remember us all being in the same house. My brothers are older and were married by the time I really got to know them. My sister, as well, was older and left soon after. You may be glad to know that they are all well – heterosexual, married, with two boys each, and living happily ever after. So I spent most of my growing up years pretty much as an only child. A child who moved through these small towns trying to fit in, trying to be normal, trying to please parents, and trying to grow up. Not an easy task for a short, severely near-sighted, crooked-toothed preacher's daughter. Particularly not for one who, looking back, knows she's been a dyke for many, many years.

That's pretty much me. My story. Or at least a working picture. There will be bits here and there that I will add. A few interesting sidenotes, a reflection or two on the pool which I have found myself at various times paddling in, or have tried like hell to swim in. Never was much of a swimmer. As a kid I used to go skinny dipping in the creek or maybe some rich friend's pool. But swimming then consisted of splashing about in the water, playing games in it, or doing the best cannon-ball dive. I have yet to understand how some people can go swimming for exercise! It simply does not fit into my concept of swimming. The thought of moving from one side of the pool to the next, assuming the water will hold you up, is amazing to me. It seems insane to think that water won't engulf you at some point. I hate swimming now, I always feel like I am going to drown. So I will tell you about the creek, about home, about a place I am from but never felt a part of, a place that is me but is now, in so many respects, so far from me. It is a splashing into the past, an articulation of stories people define their lives by, of values that I once frolicked in and now am amazed didn't engulf me.

NOTES

1 The term "religion" is obviously more encompassing than Southern Protestant Christianity. However, the American South is so permeated by Christianity that in this particular geographical and cultural context, the terms are fairly synonymous. In short, in the Bible Belt, "you either got religion or you don't." Unsurprisingly, social inclusion often depends upon whether or not one is a Christian. Other religions may, or may not, be respected but they are not grounds for social inclusion.

2 J. Bristow, *Sexuality* (London: Routledge, 1997), p. 1.

3 For further reading, see C. Pateman, *The Sexual Contract* (Oxford: Polity Press, 1988); A. Phillips, *Democracy & Difference* (University Park, Penn.: Pennsylvania State University Press, 1993); D. Coole, *Women In Political Theory: From Ancient Misogyny to Contemporary Feminism* 2nd edn (London: Harvester Wheatsheaf, 1993); L. Dominelli, *Women Across Continents: A Feminist Comparative Social Policy* (London: Harvester Wheatsheaf, 1991).

4 Certainly what distinguishes the American South as the Bible Belt is this proliferation of conservative Christianity, the bedrock of the Christian Right. So having established the context of the book, further references to the Christian Right, while being generally applicable to a larger religious–political movement, are arguably particularly potent in the South. For further discussion of the impact of Christian Right politics, see S. Bruce, *The Rise and Fall of the New Christian Right: Conservative Protestant Politics in America 1978–1988* (Oxford: Clarendon Press, 1990); and especially D. Herman, *Rights of Passage* (Toronto: Toronto University Press, 1994).

5 *Roe* v. *Wade*, 410 US 113 (1973).

6 B. Bryson, *The Lost Continent: Travels in Small Town America* (London: Abacus, 1990).

7 J. Rawls, *A Theory of Justice* (Oxford: Oxford University Press, 1972). For an example of further commentary on Rawls' work, see N. Daniels (ed.), *Reading Rawls* (Oxford: Blackwell, 1985); C. Kukathas and

P. Pettit, *Rawls: A Theory of Justice and its Critics* (Oxford: Polity Press, 1990); S. M. Okin, *Justice, Gender, and the Family* (New York: Basic Books, 1989); I. M. Young, *Justice and the Politics of Difference* (Princeton, NJ: Princeton University Press, 1990).

8 I. M. Young, *Justice and the Politics of Difference*, pp. 157–8.

9 Of course socialists, or those labeled in the South as "communists," are not the only ones who question the progressiveness of capitalism. For example, ecologists argue that because capitalism is essentially about consuming, and the world simply does not have an endless supply of resources, capitalism will soon lead us into crisis. Rather than being progressive, it is destructive. For further reading, see A. Dobson, *Green Political Thought* (London: Routledge, 1990); M. Bookchin, *The Ecology of Freedom* (Palo Alto: Cheshire Books, 1982); R. Attfield, *The Ethics of Environmental Concern* (Oxford: Blackwell, 1983).

10 The term "patriarchy" carries with it tremendous political baggage. I use it cautiously here to refer simply to the fact that men have more political, economic, and social power. For those interested in further definitions, see Z. Eisenstein, *The Radical Future of Liberal Feminism* (London: Longman, 1981); K. Millett, *Sexual Politics* (London: Virago, 1977); B. Smith, *Toward A Black Feminist Criticism* (Trumansburg, NY: The Crossing Press, 1980); S. Walby, *Theorizing Patriarchy* (Cambridge: Polity, 1990).

Chapter Two

SOUTHERN BORN AND SOUTHERN BRED

So God created man in his own image. (Genesis 1:27)

For the husband is the head of the wife as Christ is the head of the church, his body, and is himself its Savior. (Ephesians 5:23)

One of my fondest childhood memories is chatting with Mr Brown. When I was about eight years old we moved to a small town in the Texas Panhandle where, like most places, the parsonage sat only a stone's throw from the church. In between it and the church, just back from the road was his small wooden A-framed house with an overgrown elm tree in the front yard. Every night without fail, Mr Brown sat under his tree in a beat-up wicker chair, smoking roll-ups and enjoying the stillness of evening. Many of those evenings I joined him under that elm tree for a visit. He was a tall, lanky cowboy, somewhere between sixty and a hundred. He drove an old blue Ford pickup, hunting dogs riding in the back, and a couple of rifles hung up behind the seat. His boots were made of well-worn leather, as was his face. To be honest, I don't remember most of what we talked about ... a few hunting stories, complaints about the Ford's engine ... that sort of thing. Mr Brown never attended our church, but he had "fixed" it. He knew every inch of plumbing, paint and plaster in it. Mrs Brown was rarely mentioned. Once he told me about when they met, once about when she died. Both times he spoke with tears in his eyes. They had five girls. Mr Brown had raised them on his own. Bobbie, the youngest, was in high school and she, like most teens, was a source of worry. I remember when he sold his pickup and bought her an old car so she could go out with friends. But it was an old wreck, and she wouldn't be seen in it. Soon after that he got rid of the dogs, I never saw the guns again either. Bobbie eventually graduated and got married. On one of my last evenings with Mr Brown he told me that his job was complete – he had raised his girls, like he promised Mrs Brown. Not long after that he died of cancer.

Over a few beers, I tell British mates about Southern men – those sexist, racist, gun-toting red necks. Bar stories are easy to spin and are fun because they resonate with stereotypes about the South. Such stories might describe Mr Brown, but they are not a complete picture. When I step back from "gender theory," when I rein in my cynicism about the oppressive constructions of gender in my homeland, when I shut my eyes and think about what it means to be a man in the South, I picture that old cowboy sitting under the elm tree telling me about his life. Listening to the voices in this chapter you will hear sexism, racism, praise of guns, country and, of course, God. It would be so easy to stop there with such selective hearing. But alongside these words there is a sense of responsibility, a sense of struggle, a sense of what it takes to be a man.

Each man's voice heard here pays homage to an image of Southern manhood. They testify to the uniqueness of this social context in which (white) manhood is understood in essentialized terms – as a biological given, as racially evolutionary, and as a Biblical Truth. In *Men's Lives*, a text devoted to the similarities and differences of men's experience of masculinity, the writers note that while there is not a universal, essentialized "masculinity" one can locate a normative concept of masculinity within a particular social context.[1] Such a concept posits an image of the *normal* man "as the marker against which other masculinities are measured."[2] So while any presumed "essence of man" is context dependent, within a given context it may be possible to locate a normative concept of masculinity. In reflecting upon themselves, men in this chapter summon such an image. It is an image of "real" manhood so imbedded in the South's social consciousness that it affects these men's construction of "self." Descriptions of events in their lives were self-selected because they proved, for example, how protective they were, how sexy, how white, or how religious.

16

This is not to say that every Southern male is a *real* man, or completely embodies this essentialized image – although I might be shot for such blasphemy south of the Mason–Dixon line. Every man I spoke with was significantly different from every other man. Each was differently situated in relation to this image of manhood – their stories reflect their age, occupation, family status, and skin color. The distance between the image and their own varied positions irritates and disappoints, either because they cannot be the image or because they feel compelled to try. So while they speak of guns, of boots and of women, they also hint at the frustration of not measuring up – of not being the head of the household, of not being able to find a job to support their family, of not being what Southern rural culture, and the Bible, tell them they should be. My attempt to capture a glimpse of manhood in the South reveals the ease of invoking an image and the difficulty of living the reality.

BOYHOOD

One of the common denominators of men's experiences is a boy's initial encounter with social norms about what it is to be a man. Social psychologist Roger Brown captures the significance of a boy's transition to manhood:

> In the United States, a *real* boy climbs trees, disdains girls, dirties his knees, plays with soldiers, and takes blue for his favorite color. When they go to school, real boys prefer manual training, gym, and arithmetic. In college the boys smoke pipes, drink beer, and major in engineering or physics. The real boy matures into a "man's man" who plays poker, goes hunting, drinks brandy, and dies in the war.[3]

This image of boyhood is not dissimilar from my own memories of (tom)boyhood. Growing up in the South can be heaven: summer afternoons swimming in the creek, late July evenings playing little league baseball while the sun sets in the biggest sky you've ever seen, first job as a soda jerk at Mr Cherry's drug store, small schools where a graduating class of 15 is large. All of these memories paint

17

my past as a happy, Tom Sawyer childhood. But sometime, about the age of 13, I realized things were changing, and my life would never be the same. Puberty for a baby butch in a small rural community is hell. Suddenly girls were supposed to become young women, preferably cheerleaders. Okay, I tried that at a very early age but soon realized one could either be a cheerleader or study ... the former attracted boys, the latter put them right off. The entire focus of other girls' lives had changed – one summer Sherrie and I were playing baseball with the guys, the next she had a Farrah Fawcett haircut and was dating the pitcher. I never quite got over that. Guys, on the other hand, got to continue playing sports, they developed deep voices and wore jeans to church. At the time, boyhood just looked so much easier, and a lot more fun. But according to those I interviewed, this transitional period comes with a confusing mixture of dreams, family responsibilities, and expectations of manhood. The three stories below in particular tell how such expectations can shape, and shatter, those boyhood dreams.

On the Texas plains it is still common for boys to grow up on a farm 10 or 15 miles from town. In the past this social isolation caused families to become the focus for moral, and gender, development. Responsibility to parents, to the farm, and to extended family members was instilled from an early age. Jake, whose father owned a fairly large ranch nearly 20 miles from town, recalls his high-school years in the late 1940s:

> My dad was one of those that worked from 5.30 in the morning til 7.30 at night. He had two different jobs ... I was one of the more fortunate kids [because] when it came time for football practice we had to go all the way across town to the field and I was the only one in school that had any kind of a vehicle – an old, old decrepit pickup. I hauled the whole football team to the field ... And then weekends, for me, through high school were spent working at the ranch. My dad was very limited on help at that time – right at the end of World War II. There was just no people available. So he saved up all the stuff that took more than one person for Saturday morning. And right after football [games on a Friday night] that

was tough to get up at 5.00 a.m. But anyway that was the way it was for me during high school – to work at the ranch on Saturdays. And we went to church and Sunday school on Sundays.

Helping out on the ranch was a family tradition, and continues to be:

> My grandad came here in 1900 and established the ranch ... We've been out there ever since. But at the time of the war, my grandad's son and two of his nephews ... had worked at the ranch ... and they got killed in the war, all three of them. [So there wasn't anyone left to do the work.] We moved back ... because someone had to run the place. It was in a terrible mess. That's why I had to get up every Saturday morning and help fix fences ... everything was a mess during the war. But we have had the ranch forever.

Jake lived next door to me when I was in high school. He was the mayor of our small town and his wife wrote, edited, printed, and owned the local paper. Jake's brother still lives on the ranch. He and his boys work the ranch and soon it will fall to his grandkids. Jake's father now lives in the local nursing home and every morning Jake goes to help him shave and get dressed. Jake's eldest son, recently qualified as a preacher, leads the local congregation every Sunday morning. While I lived in that town for only a couple of years, his family certainly made an impact on my life. Like so many other rural communities, a few families have been there forever and therefore will remain the power of the community forever. If you are lucky enough to be born into one of those families, the security of that inherited power makes it tempting to never leave. But the times, as they say, are a-changing. In today's world of mass communication, the social isolation of rural life is giving way to dreams of the outside world. The security of home and the desire to move on creates a tension for young men who struggle with both responsibilities to take care of the family and expectations to "do better."

Along some backroad in Georgia I came across a baseball diamond just a mile outside a town of about 600 people. From the road, I could see the game was well underway and, feeling a bit nostalgic for my own little league days, I decided to stop and watch a bit. Stepping out of the car, the smell of hot-dogs and popcorn enticed me toward the small group of spectators lounging in the sun on the old wooden stands. After feeding my face, and yelling at the batter to stop swinging at every pitch, I decided to have a chat with the nice middle-aged couple behind me. It was one of those occasions where everyone there knew everyone else, and no one knew me. At least I think that explains their initial suspicion. I thickened my Southern tongue and introduced myself. Pulling out my card, proving academic credentials, I told them about my journey across the South to research the culture of my homeland. Barbara and Gary were suitably impressed and, having decided I was not an ax-murderer, agreed to talk with me a while. Gary had grown up here, learned how to be a mechanic from his father, and married Barbara just after high-school graduation. His son Tom was the pitcher for the local team and wanted to go to college on a baseball scholarship. Given that he was only 13 and that the high school had no baseball program, his dreams of the Big League were probably never going to amount to much. But he wasn't telling Tom that just yet. "Boys gotta dream. Reality sets in soon enough. He helps me in the shop sometimes. I hate to tell him that's where he is likely to spend the rest of his life." Barbara, a hairdresser, glanced at me, "Oh he'll go to college. If I have to do every person's hair in this county until I am 75. He'll go to college." After a couple of innings it was clear to me she might just have to do that. Tom couldn't hit the broad side of a barn much less the catcher's mitt. Gary offered me a beer and toward the end of the game I asked if I might be able to talk with Tom. After a rather strange look between them, and me promptly reassuring them that we could sit right here in full view, they agreed.

Tom wasn't too thrilled at first, but I waited until all his friends left and then began by asking him about the game. He said the team now had a 1 and 9 record. They had beaten only one other team all summer but had one game left so maybe they could make it two. Then I asked him about school and the future:

I hate school. Well, I like sports and am pretty good at English. I like to read – westerns, sci-fi, history, anything really. No, that's not true. I picked up one of mom's Harlequins [romance novels] once. Yuck! But yeah, I'd like to go to college. I don't know what I want to be, but I don't want to be here forever. No money around here. No jobs. Mom and dad never have enough. I try to help dad out but I don't want to work on cars for the rest of my life.

Tom looked a bit uneasy, hesitated then added, "Not that dad's a bad mechanic, he's got a way with cars, can fix anything. It's just that they work so hard. Never have much time for anything else." He hadn't mentioned the dreams about baseball stardom so I pushed him a bit more:

Course I dream about playing in college. But I ain't stupid. I ain't got no chance of that, not coming from this little place. Would be nice to get a scholarship though. Mom really wants me to get to college. And I do too, but I know how things are. They ain't got the money and so I'd have to have a scholarship. If I don't get one, I guess I'll just stay around here for a while, maybe work for dad until I can afford it on my own ... I want to see the world, travel ... to get out of here ... if I can't go to college, maybe I will join the army ... I just don't want to be here for all my life.

Tom seemed pretty mature for his age, so I decided to test the waters and inquire about a girlfriend. His face turned three shades of red and he let out an embarrassed attempt at laughter. Now I am certain that 13-year-old boys talk about girls, but not to a stranger, particularly a strange woman. No he didn't have a girlfriend; of course he had kissed a girl; no he hadn't had sex; yes he would get married some day; could we stop now? I walked him to his parents' car and thanked them.

I will never know what happens to Tom. He may go to college. Without money or sufficient education, he may join the army like so many others trying to get away from rural life. Dreaming of a world beyond the city limits, more and more young people pack their bags after high-school graduation and head off to find "life" somewhere else. I passed through hundreds of rural communities each one marked by boarded up town squares and derelict houses. This life used to offer security: for raising a family, for jobs, for the American Dream. Now fulfilling that dream seems to lead somewhere else, anywhere else. One man in Tennessee told me about the security of his boyhood:

> Well, [I'm in] the automotive industry. And it used to be ... when we were growing up, we all knew that we ... kind of like ... communism in a sense ... we knew what we were going to do when we grew up. We all knew we were going to work at the steam plant, which is our power plant out here. We knew we were going to work there, that was it. "What are you going to do when you grow up?" "I'm going to work for TVA [Tennessee Valley Authority]." "Me too." Your dad worked for TVA. Uncle worked for TVA. Everyone works for TVA. That's where we're going to be. You know, and you could always see the stack where the steam plant is, anywhere in this county you went, you'd look and say, "that's where I'm going to work." But it didn't turn out.

Fortunately for him, an automotive factory opened up just outside the town and he eventually found work there. Having found job security, he appears to have a fondness for rural life. But his affection is somewhat tainted by the restrictions accompanying this simplicity:

> Everything is pretty much peaceful here ... if you get something like a car wreck, now that's big news on the front page of the paper. A car wreck, or maybe somebody killed in an accident by [a] tree falling on him, or something like that. You can live in this town, right downtown, and still have room to breathe and not be pressured by city life, because it's not that rat racy here. Now, as a matter of fact they will ask me at work tomorrow who was that girl I was talking to ...
>
> My brother ... he PhD'd at Vanderbilt and got the hell out of here. He's Republican now ... I don't know the difference. All I know is the American Dream – well here the Dream is find a good job, get your ass off the farm and don't look back. Don't look back

... All I want to do is work, make a decent living, pay my child support, retire at about fifty or sixty five ...

I always had a saying: there were three things that you can have in life, but you can never have more than two of them – that's time, money and ability. So from the time of birth until we get up into the working world, we have all the time and all the ability we want, but we have no money, until we start working. Now we have money, and we have ability, but we have no time, because we have our nose to the grindstone. Then we retire, we've got money and time, but no ability.

Each of these three stories illustrate how boyhood dreams may be shaped by family responsibilities or by the economic restrictions of rural life. Each of them represents a different generation's attempt to negotiate what it means to become a man. For Jake growing up in the 1940s, the American Dream was working on the farm and raising his children within these family traditions. Rural life offered a good job and a safe home for his family. The man from Tennessee struggled as a teen in the 1960s to understand what it was to "be a man." We will meet him again in the next section as "Bubba." First, I think maybe it is important to hear the disappointment in his voice. For him the American Dream seems to have changed before his eyes. While growing up, life looked easy, sorted, stable. But when he was ready to take it on, the goal posts had moved. No longer did a man get a local job and raise a family. Instead the Dream was to get away, like his brother. In middle age, his fortress against this disillusionment is a fierce pride in "Dixie" and an even stronger hatred of those he blames for such change. It is important to contextualize this disappointment as later we hear nothing but hostility from this "Bubba."

The story that tugged at my heart was that of Tom. When I graduated from high school there were about a dozen boys in my class. As far as I know, two of them made it to college, a couple have stayed at home, and the rest joined the army. The quality of rural education, and the price of higher education in America, has made the military the only way out of rural isolation. "Be all you can be. See the world with the Army." At only 13, Tom is painfully well aware of the limited options for his life. In a few years, or perhaps already, his fading dreams of a baseball career will give way to the reality of life as a mechanic or enlisted man. I am still convinced that boyhood in a rural community is fun. I am equally aware that such Mark Twain simplicity often limits life chances both in terms of economic opportunity and appropriate expressions of gender.

"MOMMAS DON'T LET YOUR BABIES GROW UP TO BE COWBOYS"

As portrayed by Hollywood or Ralph Lauren, the cowboy image is the ultimate in sexy butchness. Maybe that's why I have always thought that there is something inherently attractive about cowboys. Not that I have conducted a complete survey of every cowboy in the South, or even all of them in Texas, but I have known a few. Trust me, these guys are butch – Saturday night, heavily starched Levi jeans and equally crisp shirt, leather belt with "bull riders do it best" buckle, and of course, boots and a Stetson hat. Driving the pickup, singing to George Strait, cruising slowly through town sipping a Coors. Such cowboys figure predominantly in my memories of life in rural Texas. Even my own affection for boots emerged after I realized that I, too, could lead a cowgirl around the dance floor. Similarly most Southern boys growing up in rural communities have first-hand knowledge of the heroic image of the cowboy, the "embodiment of the American spirit":

> Ideally, the cowboy is fierce and brave, willing to venture into unknown territory and tame it for its less-than-masculine inhabitants. As soon as the environment is subdued though, he must move on, unconstrained by the demands of civilized life, unhampered by clinging women and whining children. The cowboy is a man of impeccable ethics, whose faith in natural law and natural right is eclipsed only by the astonishing fury with which he demands adherence to them. He moves in a world of men, in which daring, bravery, and skill are constantly tested.[4]

Undoubtedly the spirit of the cowboy can still be found in the rural

South. Like Jake in the previous section, Joe still lives in his hometown. His family owned a large ranch and did a bit of farming on the side. When he was 22, he was traveling the rodeo circuit as a bull rider. His body and heart still carry the scars of broken limbs and broken dreams of life on the circuit. Along the way he fell in love with Julia, a local rodeo queen who looked like a model.

> She was so beautiful. And, well, no one ever accused me of being handsome. But somehow I got her to go out with me. We both loved the country life. We both loved the Lord. And before long I knew that I would have to return home, marry her and settle down. We got a couple of great kids now. I get up early and go to the farm. She does a bit of work locally. We are both dedicated to the community, to the local school, and to the church ... Sometime I dream about what my life would have been like if I had stayed on the circuit. I was pretty good. But my old body had had enough ... Yeah, I am a cowboy ... I even play a bit of country music on my guitar ... but it's about working on the land, raising a good family.

Talking with Joe was like pulling teeth – cowboys aren't known for sharing their feelings. What does come through in his few words is the way in which he has adopted the image of the rough-and-ready cowboy to the needs, and responsibilities of his own life. He had tamed nature – in the rodeo as well as on the farm and ranch. Now, in his mature years, he is that "man of impeccable ethics" as a leader in the community, the church, and provider for his family.

However, on the rest of my journey across the South I found that such cowboys are a dying breed. More often than not, young cowboys find their "wilderness" in the Country and Western bar where one's "skill" at hunting is tested by the "game" of a beautiful cowgirl. And courage comes in a bottle or a pill. Talking about sex with these guys often involved references to hunting – to capturing and conquering – of the weak. Sex is clearly about power. Correspondingly, rural young women know that cowboys, particularly after a few beers, "naturally" will do whatever it takes to get sex. When gender norms, supported with Biblical references, mandate women as "submissive" and men as "deserving," sex is definitely about power. Saturday night in a pickup decorated with weapons and parked out on a dirt road, "no" does not mean "no."

While I met this contemporary "cowboy" in almost every bar and bar-b-que from Georgia to Texas, I was concerned that my increasing cynicism could obscure this research. So I decided to go out with a cousin of mine and a few of his friends to see if a bit of repositioning could enlighten me as to the more positive aspects of these contemporary cowboys. Really, what did women see in these guys?

It had been a long time since I went out two-stepping with a guy, and even longer since I went out with a group of them for some male bonding. My first mistake was to assume that just because "cuz" owned a pickup and a Stetson, we would go two-stepping. I changed clothes and we left for the disco. My second mistake was to assume a dyke could do male bonding. Of course I felt safe with my cousin, and even enjoyed checking out the long-legged Texas women with him. But after a few beers, and cocktails, and whatever the boys were on, the conversation slipped beyond admiring women to the seriousness of the "kill." Women became things to possess, to have for the night, to fuck and throw away. For example, one guy, who had insisted on wearing his cowboy gear to the disco, explained how one knows if a girl is of legal age: "You stick her in a barrel, if she's tall enough to see out, she's old enough. If she isn't, you cut off the barrel." By the time I had witnessed my cousin dancing his rooster strut – supposedly a sure girl catcher – I was ready for home. Reflecting upon this experience, I will not make a third mistake by assuming these contemporary cowboys are simply sexist bastards. They are small-town guys away from home and what they want most in life is a good job, a good woman and a few bucks for beer. They are simply struggling to be "men." Verbally belittling "other" women is an obvious attempt to find and assert power. Since that night, I have watched them interact with "not so other" women, and while they do attempt to assert power, when it comes to girlfriends and family the boys love and respect them. Indeed, they treated me brilliantly. But then again, I am family. Not only that, I am the family dyke, one who likes girls – just like they do. Well, not quite.

I will admit that my night out with the boys was most disappointing because we didn't go country dancing. I get few chances in England to wear my boots and do a bit of two-stepping. But my night out did highlight the selective use of the cowboy gear to plug into the Southern rural butchness. Like the required boots and hat, it is something one can put on, an image one can invoke through costume and attitude. Few guys actually work on a ranch or ride in rodeos. Nevertheless, the commercialization of the cowboy culture entices them to assume the image. Our man from Tennessee, Bubba, is fed up with it:

Cowboy boots? I don't wear cowboy boots and I don't wear a cowboy hat – for the fact that I never rode a cow in my life. That [country music] kind of got out of hand. Nashville went too commercial. I mean it's bad, it's *real* bad. You've got people who moved here just for the fact that they wanted to live near Nashville. We've got people strolling out here, and they're from somewhere else, because they want to make it in the music business. I lived here all my life and I can play, I write songs, I sing, I do the whole shooting match, but I've never had no desire to go to the Grand Ol' Oprey ... because it's been drummed in my head all my life. I mean these people are going crazy over Nashville, country music and line dancing. And I'm thinking, my God, [when you've] lived with it all your life ... Everybody is coming here and they don't understand we're trying to get up enough money where we can leave!

A friend of mine, came here from Oregon. I worked with him, got to know him, hung out with him for about three years. His wife was into song writing. She moved from Oregon, and came all the way here to be closer to Nashville, because she wanted to promote some of her music. And I told him, when he first told me that was the reason why he was here, I said, "Mistake No. 1, there's too much competition here." You take a good country band in Oregon and you can pay the rent. But you can't do it here, because you can't play a bar like this for 50 bucks on a Friday or Saturday night. That ain't going to get it. But if you go some place where there is none, where there's a bunch of northern accents and you'll play every night and people will love it.

I wrote him a song when he left. He went back to Oregon, tucked his tail and left ... it wasn't happening here. And a line of that song was:

> "You say the grass is greener, the sky is bluer, you've got better taste in beer. But if everything's so good up there, what the hell you are doing here? Now we can't even have a conversation, because you know everything and then some. You just take your Yankee ass right back where you came from."

Now, let me tell you about meeting Bubba. One afternoon I was driving through the Tennessee countryside, stopping once in a while to visit with the locals, when I came upon a country bar set just outside the city limits of some small town. Usually this means that the city fathers have decided that there should be no bars in the city, so bars sprout up just far enough out of town for people to have to drive home drunk. At least it keeps the sin of alcohol away from the good people of "Podunk." I decided to stop for a quick drink. A "lady" on her own should never walk into a strange (heterosexual) bar, but it was the middle of the afternoon, what could happen? I swear when I stepped through the door the music stopped and everyone in the place – all ten men – looked me up and down. While my mind was flashing pictures of gang rape on the pool table, my eyes caught sight of the one woman behind the bar. She smiled. I breathed out and moved onto a bar stool. The cold beer was nice but the cold atmosphere was still a bit scary. When she had a minute I quietly explained my mission: to speak with a few locals about growing up near the country music capital. We both turned and surveyed the options: four old fellas playing cards amidst a table of beer cans, a couple of guys shooting pool, another couple whispering in the corner, and two glued to the computer game at the end of the bar. "Bubba," she shouted so everyone turned and stared, "this here girl wants to interview someone, you want to talk to her?" His eyes never left the game, he just said "in a minute."

While waiting for Bubba to shoot all the aliens, I gave him the once over – about 6′3″, three hundred pounds, red hair, and a beard down to his belly. The army hat I didn't actually notice until later. Bubba was a researcher's dream: he had opinions on everything.

And he had a few surprises. Fortunately he liked me, or liked talking. At first his dislike for Yankees I took to come from his cultural pride about country music. Pretty soon, I realized that music had little to do with it. And that Yankee cowboys were the least of his concerns.

Bubba is a middle-aged, white, working-class Southern man. Since his boyhood in the 1950s, this is probably the one group who has been the most systematically disempowered in America. The technological revolution and global economy have taken away the assumed job stability. The American Dream is no longer about a good job in a small town. It is about getting an education so one can leave. Economic power is elsewhere and inaccessible. Anti-discrimination laws and affirmative action have called into question the Southern white's evolutionary right to superiority. The "government," a dirty word in many a Southern heart, has taken too much away. "They" have neither respected white men's rights nor their right to defend their power when threatened. The right to defend oneself, to bear arms, is guaranteed by the American Constitution. Probably not disconnected from this, the gun is the most recognized signifier of power associated with men. In the hands of a "real country man," moreover in the hands of a true Confederate rebel like Bubba, it is the (only) means by which men can defend against challenges to power. There are thousands just like him across the South taking up arms against those who threaten their "rightful" power.

I'm a gun dealer. Around here that is something you are supposed to do. You grow up with it all your life. There was always two things you can associate in every home ... the majority of homes around here ... the home I grew up in ... there was always a gun and there was always a guitar. Well you had to. If you didn't play the guitar you were the black sheep of the family.

Militias are strong in Tennessee. Matter of fact, I'm in a militia. I'm in the Alliance of the New World Confederacy. It's an organization designed ... a peace-loving organization designed to preserve and protect the American way of life, liberty and the pursuit of happiness. It's in the Constitution. And you don't fight amongst

yourselves, you fight everybody else. You know, 200 years ago ...
300 years ago ... militias at one time were called minutemen, and
everybody loved having one next-door. They thanked God they had
a minuteman living next-door to protect us from the British. OK?
And now you say "Militia," oh no, its taboo, get rid of it, burn it
down ... like Waco.

Well the only thing we knew there about David Koresh in Waco,
Texas was what the media had told us. We watched on the news and
of course the media is always going to right the opposite. They
drum it in to the public's head what [they think] is going on. First
they told us, "we've got a child molester at Waco, Texas who has
barricaded himself inside the house with a thousand automatic
rifles." Well, what they didn't know, or didn't tell the public, was
that every automatic rifle that David Koresh had was registered as
an automatic rifle ... was bought through a gun dealer, proper
paperwork filled out. What had happened was that he'd got too
many and built up a bank and it scared people. It scared the government ...

And Oklahoma, I think [the] Oklahoma bombing was, in my own
opinion, was an inside job. I think the ATF [Bureau of Alcohol,
Tobacco and Firearms] or some people who originally worked for
ATF had done it, because ... look at the facts. The ATF building,
their offices were on the third floor. The bomb was set on the opposite end of the building. OK? Now ATF people were told they did
not have to come to work the next day [the day of the bombing]. I
mean all the officers were told "You don't have to come to work,
you're off tomorrow." But they didn't tell the office people, the jani-
tors, the daycare people. They didn't tell nobody else in the building.
They told the ATF officers, "Do not come to work tomorrow." And
the poor guy Timothy McVeigh, who was supposed to take the rap
for it ... if he'd really have done that, then why would he be driving
away from the scene in an automobile with no license plates? Why
would he be speeding away? You'd think he would want to make it
out of town as quietly and inconspicuously as possibly. OK? And if
he was such the brutal killer that he was, why didn't he kill the lone
highway-patrol man who stopped him? I mean he just took out 300
people, what's one more?

Well it was something else we will never know ... like Kennedy,
OJ, Waco, Oklahoma, you never know. Well somebody will come

forward a few years from now, an old man and say, "I done it."
He'll have all the proof, all the documentation, but it won't matter
then. What would we do? Give him the chair if he is 86 years old?

When I was about 14 my sister and her boyfriend, Henry, used to let
me go coyote hunting with them. At night Henry would drive the
pickup slowly down dirt roads while I stuck my hand out the
window shining a huge spot light on the hillside. Supposedly when
the light hit a coyote, its eyes would glimmer in the light long
enough for Henry to stop the truck, grab his gun and expertly nail
him. Looking back I remember two things: that my sister got to ride
in the middle catching all the warmth from the heater while I froze
by the open window, and the crack of the gun echoing through the
cab of the truck. Needless to say, Henry never actually hit a coyote.
It was probably some ploy of theirs to get mom and dad to let them
stay out late. Of my 20 or so years in rural Texas, that is my only
memory of actual gunfire. Since the "incident" in Waco and the
Oklahoma bombing, such naiveté is no longer possible, or even
desirable.

As the "embodiment of the American spirit" the cowboy, it has
been said, "is a man of impeccable ethics, whose faith in natural
law and natural right is eclipsed only by the astonishing fury with
which he demands adherence to them."[5] This heroic image may
serve as one of sexy butchness, or even sexist honor. But certainly
there is something terrifying in the transition from that historical
idealism to contemporary vigilantism. The anger, the fury, of
Bubba has been ignited by what he perceives as a disregard for
natural law and natural rights. The older cowboys may have seen
their day, the younger ones may continue to play in their costumes
even if they can't follow in their footsteps. But this generation in
the middle, the ones who were brought up idealizing country life
only to find it both devalued and appropriated for fun by outsiders,
the ones full of anger, are festering in the American South. The
proliferation of guns, and militia groups, is only compounded by
the most frightening social disease rooted deeply in Southern
culture: racism.

WHITE IS RIGHT

The only vacation I can remember our family taking was the summer mom and dad and I drove through the South. Literally, we drove for two weeks along a zillion dirt roads from Texarkana to Atlanta. Sleeping in the back of a van, eating baked bean sandwiches. We stopped twice: at Graceland and at Opreyland. Oh, and on Sunday, we stopped to go to church. It's funny how at 13, the two weeks took almost forever and now I can't recall much of what we did or even talked about. What I can still picture however, is the labels "Black" and "White" separating the communal space: everything from bathrooms to churches. Of course, at the time I didn't really think much about it. I had grown up in the midst of people associating labels of "nigger" with "dirty," "lazy," "bad," "frightening," etc. But then I went away to college. I moved on – into a world that did not make such assumptions, at least publicly. Every time I return to the South I am shocked at the continued imbeddedness, the normalcy, of racism – at the way in which racism is simply never questioned, never even noticed, by the majority of the white population. The time I spent researching for this book only confirmed what I had feared: the Confederacy is alive and well.

In this section I want to consider briefly the manifestations of racism in the lives of three men. Before I do that however, I need to account for my selection of their voices. First, as I have mentioned in the introduction, the methodology for this research limited the amount of Black people I spoke with in the South. The majority of the population living in poverty in the South are African-Americans and Latinos. I have no doubt that if I had spoken with more, this section could have been better balanced, particularly in terms of class. Given this, Paul's story, as a middle-class Black man, should not be assumed to speak for all Black Southern men. However, I have included it at the end of this section because it is the antithesis of what white racists *expect* to be the story of all Black Southern men.

Second, this is the only point at which I explicitly address racism in this book. That should not be taken as an indication that racism can only be associated with white men. Southern white women are racist, although I think slightly less violent. Racism also plays an interesting role in the abortion debate. And, even in the more "tolerant" gay and lesbian community, racism often settles itself quietly under our political correctness. So while it may be mentioned in the remaining chapters, by focussing on it here I am trying to offer a realistic account of its fury.

Finally, I have began this section with two white voices which testify to their readiness to use violence to express this fury. The white male voices of anger, of violence, record the Confederacy's inability to deal positively with the legacy of slavery. Black people in the rural South, as in many American industrial urban centers, have been blamed for the flagging economy, the scarcity of jobs for whites, the rising crime rate, the alarming incidence of violence. It is in the South that such anger is routinely given credence – it is in the South that white men fundamentally believe their natural rights guaranteed by the Confederacy have been usurped by the Yankee government in recognizing the rights of Black people. In the face of isolation and poverty, rural Southern whites remember the glory of Dixie and, consciously or unconsciously, place the blame for the loss of such glory on the Black "other."

The extremist, Bubba, is given a substantial amount of space. Probably many Southerners would like to deny he still exists. But he does. And quite frankly, he was very easy to find. The second voice is that of the more subtle, more "socially acceptable" racism. George's words are the familiar language *every* Southerner continues to take for granted, or to expect, in day-to-day conversation. He tells about growing up in a small segregated community where violence against young Black men was an accepted norm. And about the friendships that emerged once he got to know the Black "other." The last voice could have been included in the final "religion" section of the chapter. Paul is a committed father, a loving husband, and as a teacher he is a part of the growing Black middle class. His notion of manhood is firmly patterned upon Biblical fatherhood. As a lay minister he is dedicated to empowering Black men through a ministry of encouragement, love, and hope.

Paul's answer to racial oppression suggests the fundamental importance of Biblical constructions of gender to understanding Southern
culture. But first let's hear what Bubba's got to say:

> The majority of the poverty stricken area is Black. And now you are
> hitting on a touchy subject. Because I am Southern born and South-
> ern bred. And Blacks here, they take the government for granted.
> They can get anything they want, providing they stay home, stay
> jobless, and have kids. There are Blacks who drive better cars than I
> do. I have a [well paid] job and I've got a 1977 Toyota. But these
> people are jobless, have six kids, mother-in-law living with them,
> grandmother living with them, and drive a Lexus. Something ain't
> right.
>
> We have a theory here, that if we were to get a truck load of guns
> and a truck load of cocaine, and just dump it out in the middle of
> the Black section over there, they would annihilate themselves. They
> would be fighting over it. Because any time a shooting breaks out,
> it's a Black shooting another Black. They are animals. They don't
> know any better. Get three of them together, and you can't under-
> stand them talking. You can have a one-on-one conversation with a
> Black and he'd be talking to you like I am. Get three of them
> together and they start talking a different language. And it's the
> same all over the world.
>
> You've probably heard about the shooting we had? Well, it made
> world news. It's about a guy flying the Confederate battle flag in the
> back of his truck ... I would say not over 20. He got shot because
> he had a flag flying at the back of his truck. And they changed their
> stories since then. The [Black] guy admitted that he only shot
> because of peer pressure. The gun had jammed on him, like twice,
> while he was trying to shoot him. This [white] guy's wife had just
> given birth to twins and they were about six months old at the
> time...Well, I went to his funeral, along with thousands of other
> people. All flying the Confederate flag. I tell you it was a real
> moving funeral. You ought to have seen it. As far as you could see,
> Confederate battle flags flying. And they got up there and played
> Dixie on a harmonica. A lot of people said it was a "protest." It
> wasn't. It was a movement ... That's the kind of crack you've got to
> deal with when you deal with Blacks.
>
> It [the Confederate flag] was an emblem of the Confederacy. You

got to know why the war was fought. I mean, just like I told this guy earlier, I said, "The Southern people thought that the north were after our women." You see, we didn't lose the battle. We *quit fighting*. Because we thought they were after our women. Then we found out they were after our Blacks, and we just quit fighting. Give up.

There are Blacks across the tracks. Now, this is a white section, always has been, since I was a little fella. But now we have Blacks living here, within 300 feet. Middle class. But what they're doing is they're trashing the neighborhood. You know, it was a nice neighborhood. I don't know what it is associated with Blacks and four cars, but they will put four that don't work in their back yard. And they are just trashing the damn neighborhood.

Do you know how many people missed work the day of the Million Man March? Two. Right? Two out of a million niggers had a job. Well, you watch. That will be a recognized holiday. It will be like Martin Luther King's birthday. Now *we* won't get no time off. But the postal service will shut down, courthouse will shut down, the day of the Million Man March. Do you know what? Personally, I think we ought to celebrate James Earl Ray's birthday ... He's the man that shot Martin Luther King. Hell, he's a hero. I don't think James Earl Ray killed him. He just happened to be in the wrong place at the wrong time, driving a white convertible. The same kind of car the shot was fired from. Yes, he's a hero as far as I'm concerned. Because what would have happened if Martin Luther King had lived? I think the government stepped in on that one and said "Hey hammer him down. We can only let the Blacks go so far." Jesse Jackson will be the next one to catch a bullet, if he don't keep his mouth shut. Well, he ain't got in that deep yet. He's quiet, he's kind of backing away again. Hell, he knows it. He knows he's got crosshairs on his forehead.

But like schools, when I was growing up, I could have walked to school because I lived that close. But then this desegregation thing come along. All of a sudden I had to get on a bus and get drove right to the middle of the Black section in town and go to the Black school. And yet the Blacks got to go to my school, which I could have walked to, and he could have walked to his. Well I never did have to go to school with Black people until I got to sixth grade. I got in the sixth grade and I was shoved in this school which was

60 percent Black. And I was in a minority. A minority is *not* a majority.

[Now] my eight-year-old daughter goes to school in the Black section. And she drives by all the run-down shanties. And all the cars up on the blocks. The crack deals going on out on the street, and all this stuff, and she drives by that to school.

I never had problems [at school after desegregation]. But it did happen in the job aspect of it. Because, like I said, back at TVA [Tennessee Valley Authority], the man that lived in our neighborhood was a superintendent out there. He done the hiring and the firing at TVA. When I turned 18 and got out of high school and I went out there for a job. He told me, "There's nothing I can do right now." The government had done this. He said, "If you were a Black veteran, I could put you to work tomorrow morning. But you are an 18-year-old single, white male. Nothing I can do." Yet you had the Blacks out there, that the government gave them the jobs. You had to fill a quota of "token Blacks" ... is what we called them ... and they'd be out there leaning on their shovels all day long, not working. And there we were, couldn't get a job.

And right now I'm a middle-aged, single white man ... the biggest majority in the world right now ... I mean minority. But the white man can't holler discrimination, the Black can in a minute. Yes, yes, if you're Black you can go to work in a minute. If you're white you're kind of discriminated against, but you can't say that word because white and discrimination don't ... you're not suppose to say that in the same sentence ... there's just no such thing.

But I sold a lot of hand guns to Blacks. And I had a white friend ask me one time, "Why do you want to sell these hand guns to these Blacks?" He said, "Man, don't you know what they are going to do? They are going to rob your mama." I said, "No, if I sell a white man a hand gun, he's going to go out on Saturday afternoon shoot a few targets, shoot a few beer cans and go home, and put it back in the sock drawer. I sell a Black man a hand gun, he's going to kill another Black." My part to secure white supremacy.

I warned you, Bubba is pretty extreme. Not necessarily unusual, but extreme. He admitted to me, he wasn't a church-goer. Perhaps that is unsurprising. But then again, perhaps not. I remember a couple of my daddy's church members who belonged to the KKK. In the Bible Belt, where morality is (literally) black and white, good Southern (white) Christianity sits all too easily with Southern racism. Bubba may be more bold, but the sentiment is an all too familiar mark of the Southern whiteness. The history of racism infiltrates the social consciousness, reproducing itself through a language that clearly delineates difference. In the academic ivory tower, we theorize about the "politics of difference," about multiculturalism, about pluralism. In the South, many still struggle to recognize any basic sameness, even simple humanity.

A little ways into Alabama I stopped for gas and a cup of coffee. Sitting at the counter next to me was an older man who struck up a conversation about the quality of the coconut pie. One thing led to another and I eventually pulled out my tape recorder. George told me about his growing up, his childhood shenanigans and his "old friends":

A lot of us got together in high school, in the back end of a pickup truck, with a rubber hose about three foot long, with cement about six or eight inches on each end, and we'd drive through nigger town ... whopping niggers on the back of the head ... We had a policeman living next door to mother and dad. Him and his partner rode motor cycles and they caught us one night over in nigger town and took us back to this side of the river and told us ... "If we catch you back over there tonight we're gonna lock you up." Hell, we beat them back to nigger town. We knew they weren't going to lock us up. But we did such as that, nothing real bad.

They [Blacks] had separate schools ... let's see, when [my daughter] was in the sixth grade they started bussing, so that would be in '72 or '73 ... When she was in the eighth or ninth grade, she come home one day and said that their band director was off sick and they had this Black man teaching them. I told her, I said, "Baby I tell you what to do when you go to class in the morning, if he's there walk up and tell him, say 'How's Uncle Hal? Dad said to tell you hello.'" She looked at me kind of funny and said "Daddy you trying to get me in trouble?" I said, "No, I'm not ... but you tell him your dad said hello. OK?" She got in the truck that next afternoon, she said "Daddy, I walked up to that man and told him to bend over and I hugged his neck, called him Uncle Hal, and told him my daddy said hello. He looked at me kind of funny and said 'What's your name girl?' and I told him. And he said 'Is [name] you grand-daddy?' and I said 'Yes, sir.' She said, 'he took up half the class period talking about you and grandpa and about the cornet you gave him while you were in the service.'" I did, I gave him a cornet ... He had kids over [at the Black high school] that needed a horn to play ... Their parents couldn't afford one so I gave him mine. And she said, "Well he still remembers it." I said, "Well he should, he's known me all my life." [The daughter asked] "Well daddy, why didn't you tell me that you'd known him all your life?" I said, "You didn't ask."

There's a nigger got a service station over on the corner. I can walk in over there and take anything out of there that I want to. Not say a word to a soul just go on in there and get it, walk out with it. He'll come back and ask them [employees] ... and all them boys that work for him, tell him, "Your brother got it." Him and I threw bricks at each other when we was kids. He worked at another service station up on another corner when he was a kid. And he and I used to throw rocks, bricks, peaches ... green peaches, oh they hurt when they hit ... We've always been friends ... We were always doing something to each other, but we've stayed friends all these years.

George recalls his experience of committing physical violence towards Black boys as "nothing real bad." Over the years he believes he has made peace with the same Black boys he used to fight. But what must have been Hal's experience of "nothing real bad"? Now George wouldn't think of harming Hal, his friend. The Black boy whom he threw bricks at was an unknown – the "Black other." Such distrust, fear and hatred of the "Black other" remains the foundation for stereotypes of Black men as lazy, as drug dealers, as potentially threatening.

In a suburb outside of Atlanta I met up with Paul, a northern middle-class African-American who chose to make his home in the South. Sitting in his comfortable living room, hearing his wife preparing supper and his children watching the TV, I told him about my encounter with Bubba. I asked him about racism in the school where he is a teacher, about the Million Man March, and about the stereotypes of Black men:

> I work for the Catholic school and there's a tremendous difference between the treatment of white people and of Black people. Even in the political system, there's tremendous differences made. And within the schools. It's more prevalent here in the South than it was up North where I am from. It's different. There's so much prejudice and discrimination here, but they cover it up. They cover it up in the name of the Lord, or in the name of politics ...
>
> There's a lot of people that went there, to the Million Man March. It was a threat – a lot of employers threatened their people by saying "You can't take off." Jeopardize this, you jeopardize that. I just didn't feel the need at that time. Or that it was the call was for me. I'm already doing something positive ...
>
> I used to have the viewpoint like Bubba ... I mean, he may have been a white militia guy, but I was a Black militant guy. Like, hey, let's kill 'em out, let's get rid of them once and for all. At one time, they [racists] prompted fear, from a standpoint of what they could do to the Black race. But now there's a reciprocal anger. Because as angry as whites may be to Blacks, Blacks are as angry. They [some Black men] will kill at the drop of a hat. So, killing one another, they do that, it's there, that attitude is there ...
>
> And often, in our community, in the Black communities, the role models are Black actors in movies. I try to tell my wife all the time that they stereotype everything ... But a lot of this is not stereotypes. I guess it all depends on where you go ... In a lot of our communities the drug rate is high; the crime rate is high; there's Black on Black crime – a lot of Black on Black crime. The guys, Black men who kill other Black men, don't get arrested, you can kill one another, they [white police] don't care.

Paul recognizes the realities of this Black image and its effect on Black manhood. For him, the answer is to find a role model in God the Father. Only by returning to the family, by becoming the head of the household, by "being a man" can Black men have a hope of rising out of oppression. His "family values" grow out of his own need for a male role model and his determination to provide one for his children:

> I understand my family. I understand my kids, because I am a family guy. I came from a broken home, was raised by a single mom. I think that, my dad wasn't really there when I was growing up, so it almost hindered me from having a healthy relationship with our Heavenly Father ... I began reading the Bible and I didn't recognize that I had hurt inside of me, anger inside me. I read the Bible and I kind of deposited the information on the inside based on God and sin, that information changed my life. I really needed to release my dad because he didn't want the responsibility as the earthly father. My dad should have been just like – and every dad you know – should have been just like the Heavenly Father.
>
> I have a difficult time now, and it's not easy teaching my own boys to be responsible men. Because I know that some point in time they'll want to become one with somebody's daughter and they need to be responsible. I want to be involved, directly involved, with who my daughter's going to marry. Because I need to know if I'm dealing with a broken home, alcoholic background, drug abuse, battered children. I need to know if I'm dealing with any of that, any family curses. But, my daughters just don't feel their dad should be directly involved in that. They think they are mature and old enough to make their own decisions.
>
> [When] I leave my children home, I leave instructions for my 12-year-old son, I leave instructions for my 14-year-old boy, and I leave instructions for my 16-year-old daughter. Now, if she decides that she don't want to do what I have asked her to do and the other children follow her based on her decisions, when I come back I deal with them individually. I want to think like God, you see, God's not going to deal with me based on what you did, he's going to deal with me personally. So that's how I deal with my kids. I say, "Now, what are the instructions I left with you? What did you do? Now if you made a decision to follow her, if that's a decision that you made, it was wrong. Because she did wrong, now you did wrong, based on what was a bad decision." I challenge them to make their own decisions ...
>
> God's best was not for a single parent home. You take our homes without the male model there and it's tragic. It's tragic. It was tragic

for me. It was. We took a bad situation and a lot of good came out of it, but that was not God's best. The male and the female, that is a healthy bond where kids can be raised up. It's not an ethnic thing. This will fit anybody wherever they come from. In single parent homes, the kids come up one sided. There's more than one side, and in most families, it's the mother.

Well, I came up without a role model, a male role model. I didn't know what it was like to be a man ... I didn't know what I needed to be. I only knew from the standpoint of my ma. I didn't have positive male role models in my home. I didn't know how to be a father. I didn't know how to be a good son. It was difficult because my dad wasn't there.

Paul's faith in "God the Father" provides a path of hope out of racial oppression. His volunteer ministry in a state prison gives him the opportunity to share this with others. In the face of institutional racism, Paul believes that hope for change has to come from within each individual:

Let me say from the standpoint of me being involved with prison ministries ... In the prisons, the highest population is Black males. The next highest population is Black females. It works like that in the juvenile facilities ... It is as though the police, and I don't want to say that the Blacks are mobbed, but they'll [police] go in the neighborhood with a huge truck and they will just gather everybody on there and lock them up. I really hated to see that when I went into the institutions – very few whites, very few Orientals ... there are some ... but the highest population is Black. Once they are inside ... there is no reformation program ... as far as I have seen in the system. No, no. They're not trying to reform you.

And I was surprised to find out that ... I thought the institutions were owned by the state, or ... the federal government ... but I find out that ... the prison, it's owned by shareholders. I was shocked to find that out. It's owned by shareholders. Now, they need to fill those up so our people are rounded up. It's a business. They run it like a business, as much as they can keep people inside of those cells or those dorms, it's costing taxpayers money. It's a business.

Through the prison ministry we want [to] reach inside of an indi-

vidual and sort of talk to their hearts. We can use words to pene-
trate their flesh to do that. So what we do is we actually challenge
them ... or try to get them to understand the forcible word or right
word.

In the prison we work on attitude. They need hope to get out of
the rut they're in. Change their attitude – not to be mad with the
system. Get rid of inferiority about themselves. Deal with themselves. Be responsible. Go back into their homes. Take care of their
families. Be men.

We try to show them a picture of the Gospel. A lot of people
can't really identify with God ... We don't want to administer religion ... We want to administer hope.

Probably the two most definitive cultural characteristics of the
South are the legacy of racism and the proliferation of Christianity.
It may be that the only way to heal racial division is by finding
common ground in religion. Such efforts to "administer hope" may
begin to salve these social wounds. However, if these efforts are
based on conservative Biblical interpretations they may in turn only
intensify normative gender divisions. Men should "be men" is easily
followed by women should "be women." "The Bible tells us so."

AND GOD CREATED MAN

What the Bible tells us, according to the "Right" interpretation, is
that men and women have different roles based on gender and on,
quite frankly, the way God meant it to be. No Godly woman's life,
certainly no Godly family is complete – as God intended – without
the presence of a man – "made in His image." According to this
interpretation, the growing number of single mothers, *causally*
linked with the rising crime rate amongst young boys/men, is
indicative of the move away from "the ideal" – the intentions of
God for family life. As Paul testifies above, many feel that the lack
of positive male role models, in the form of fathers, is the key to
understanding and correcting the wayward path of young men.
Once these men are present in family life they must fulfill particular
expectations as the "head of the household." Their God-given right,

even duty, to lead women and children is the ultimate trump-card against any worldly questioning of their decisions or actions. While the world may have attempted to erode this right since the 1960s, and while it may be economically unavoidable for women's roles to extend outside the home, it should remain clear, particularly to wives, that God intended men to be the "head of the house." Years of "women's lib" has moved America, the American family, away from recognizing the rights of men. So in America, the Promise Keepers are ensuring that hundreds of thousands of men each year learn about these "rights." Their ultimate impact upon American Christianity, and society more generally, has yet to be determined. Nevertheless, as if it was needed, masculinity is having a revival.

In this section I want to note the fundamental importance of Bible Belt religious beliefs about manhood to understanding sexuality, broadly defined, in the American South. Frankly that is impossible to do in the few pages left in this chapter. Such a complete picture may not be fully revealed in the detail considered here. Nevertheless, it is crucial to keep in mind the intensity of the beliefs conveyed in the voices here. It is an intensity often retold in this book through the eyes of those affected by its exclusion rather than those insiders who acquiesced to share directly their (sexist) beliefs. I assume, "Truth" is difficult to say directly to an "academic" "intelligent" "outsider" woman. Sometimes a larger audience, or congregation, is required. So the few voices here are interwoven with sermons witnessed, and with conversations had, off the record.

This one-to-one encounter with truth was not missed through lack of trying. My travels consistently led me to the church steps of almost every little town in which I stopped. But the amount of time a rural preacher has to talk to a strange, "difficult," woman is limited. No matter how polite I was, it became obvious within the first 10 minutes that I was too far gone to "save." My thinly veiled questions were not those of one who wished to "believe." For example, somewhere in southern Tennessee, I pulled into the gravel parking lot of a picturesque Baptist church – a white wooden building complete with steeple. I had noticed a car next to the side entrance office door and assumed the preacher was "in." The initial small town suspicion set at ease, I began by asking Pastor Brian about "family" in the 1990s. Immediately he noted the necessity of fathers as positive leaders in the family:

> In this day and age, the media tells us that all men are rapists, drug dealers, wife beaters ... There are children here in this town that don't know their own father or whose dad comes home drunk every night. There was one young girl who came to this church here a few times that told me how her father wanted her to have sex with him ... and he is, well let's just say "a public official." Kids these days need positive role models. They need discipline, sure, but they also need love – a father to listen to them. They need a leader in the family, someone who can instill good Christian family values. I ain't saying that women can't help with this. Mothers are important, especially when the kids are young. But as they grow up they need a firm guide to show them the way.

In response, I agreed that my father indeed continues to have a positive impact on my life. I proceeded by inquiring about Biblical roles for mothers and fathers. Pastor Brian, opening his Bible, read to me from Ephesians 5:21–23, "Be subject to one another out of reverence for Christ. Wives, be subject to your husbands, as to the Lord. For the husband is the head of the wife as Christ is the head of the church, his body, and is himself its Savior." "That," he added, "is God's plan, all else is of the devil." My subjection, in this particular context, was not my plan. So it took a bit of courage but I moved on to a more risky topic. My fears were confirmed when before "sexuality" could follow "homo" he had asked me if I had been "saved." Momma always says "choose your battles." I left.

Such emphatic Christian beliefs are not unheard of outside the Bible Belt. Across America, and coming soon to Britain, the message of the Promise Keepers is being heard loud and clear. As one of the fastest growing men's movements in the United States, Promise Keepers challenge men to live up to their responsibilities as Christian men. Founded by Bill McCartney, former football coach at the University of Colorado, Promise Keepers began as his vision to fill football stadiums with men to train them in what it means to be Godly men. In 1995, Promise Keepers were "training" more than 700,000 men. Promise Keepers have a clearly structured conception of Christian manhood that asserts a powerful moral patriarchy. At least verbally, they do recognize the additional need for humility before God and tenderness toward others. Perhaps surprisingly, they are a cross-cultural group actively inclusive of African-American, Asian-American and Latino men. Unsurprisingly, Promise Keepers are clear about men and heterosexuality: homosexuality "violates God's design." They are supported by right-wing religious powerhouses such as evangelist Jerry Falwell, The 700 Club, and Operation Rescue.

One of the often cited speeches from the Promise Keeper's podium comes from Dallas-based evangelist, Tony Evans:

> The first thing you do is sit down with your wife and say something like this: "Honey, I've made a terrible mistake. I've given you my role. I gave up leading this family, and I forced you to take my place. Now I must reclaim that role." Don't misunderstand what I'm saying here. I'm not suggesting that you ask for your role back, I'm urging you to take it back. If you simply ask for it, your wife is likely to say no ... Your wife's concerns may be justified. Unfortunately, however, there can be no compromise here ... Be sensitive. Listen. Treat the lady gently but lovingly. But lead!

The quotation from this speech was taken from an article in *Ms. Magazine*.[6] The reporter, a lesbian in male drag, had infiltrated the all-male weekend "training" session in Georgia. Needless to say her observations are quite interesting. *But* she heard that speech as a covert participant, and as a New Yorker who had flown to the South to get a story. I heard that speech, on the radio, driving down familiar backroads in Texas, knowing that a close family member was in the stadium.

The reporter was somewhat surprised at how love-filled the gathering was – how there was little need to assert her "masculinity." One of the most moving sights I remember from summer weeks at church camp was on the final night, when most of the

45

congregation would pray at the altar. While lullabies of spiritual music filled the air, young people, many of whom were boys, reflecting upon their troubled lives would pray – for forgiveness, for love, for hope. Clinging to each other, silent tears symbolized the difficulty of recognizing their spiritual needs. A few days later, having returned to the boredom of a small town, the same guys would be doing "guy things" – drag-racing down mainstreet, antagonizing the school "fag," and trying to do it with their girlfriends in the backseat. Recognizing the need for humility before God is one thing, giving up your divine right to power is another. Groups of Christian men may offer a safe space to express "humbleness before God," or show love toward fellow men, even as the *Ms.* reporter noted, "allowing themselves to pursue a much wider spectrum of gender behavior than would ever be tolerated in most organizations of the Christian Right."[7] But what happens to those guys when they return home? When their wives "just say no"? When their co-workers think they've got just a little too much religion? Or when a close family member comes out as a lesbian?

Well, I know what happens on a personal level. We negotiate (non) discussion. We pray a lot for change. My brother for me. Me for him. And it probably helps that I live in another country. But what about those not so – blessed? The next chapter tells the stories of women who refused to be constricted by such religiously constructed gender norms. Some of whom have had a really shit life because of that refusal. But that is not to say that it is easy, although no doubt easier, for men. In fact, many of the stories in this chapter have noted the difficulty of identifying the requirements, and then becoming, a "man." Even when those requirements are spelled out in the Good Book, or at least interpreted by the pastor, they are hard to live out. West of Atlanta I ran across a Pentecostal preacher who admitted to the discrepancy between Biblical roles and contemporary reality:

> We got too many women who think that because they're in the working world they are equal in the family. That just ain't so. The Bible is clear on this. The man is the head of the household. Of

course he should treat his wife with respect ... "love them as they do themselves" ... But Ephesians 5 says clearly a wife is to [be] subject to her husband. Man was created in the image of God and women taken from him ... not the other way around.

Now of course, when I was younger and fresh out of theology school and when me and [my wife] first got married, I expected her to do the cooking and cleaning and take care of the baby. But when we got to my first church the salary wasn't too good. She took a job at the elementary school as a secretary. And after the other two kids come along, it all got too much for her. I guess I help out more now ... doing the dishes and stuff ... but that's about working together ... I am the head of the family same as I am the head of this church.

Although the preacher admits that he had altered his own habits once personally confronted with the reality of a working household, he was, according to the word of the Lord, still the head of his household.

At this juncture I wish to relay the story of one young man which I heard rather indirectly. It is not hearsay, although it is a second-hand account of a particular person's life. I know the guy and to the best of my objective observation, it is a fairly accurate picture.

Jay had a rather difficult life: parents who fought and eventually divorced; good grades but never made it through college; grew up in a small town but never made it out as his brothers had done. He married young and the couple became very active in the local evangelical church. He was the "head of his house" and his wife he treated "kindly and lovingly" but he led. After a few years, a couple of children, and innumerable worship services, he decided that God called him to become a preacher. Unfortunately, when he made this decision his local church could not support him financially and asked instead that he remain as a lay person. Within a few months he stopped attending church. His beliefs had been shaken to their foundations. While he continued to insist that he was the head of the household, the "kindly and lovingly" stuff went out the window. At the time his story was updated for me, his wife (who had remained in the church) had had enough, and he was in danger of losing his family.

There are a number of interpretations one could give to this story. Certainly among them is that he had misinterpreted what God had intended for him and should have reconsidered his call to the ministry. Or perhaps he should have changed his membership to a more financially stable church. Some might even argue that his evangelical fanaticism was as much a product of his youth as his current crisis is a product of his fortieth birthday. While I am inclined to agree with these interpretations, I can't help but wonder that if the church was less successful at providing easy answers, he would not be in this situation. Surely he became everything they told him to be – protector/provider for his family – he kept his promise. He even took them at their word in wanting to be more "Christ-like" – a preacher. When their response to him was negative it called into question every other answer they had provided. If he could not be that "man," what kind of "man" should he be?

The ease at which Pastor Brian pointed to Ephesians 5 in response to my questions about family life is the same ease at which many preachers sermonize about gender roles. Such sermons create an image of how gender and sexuality ought to be. On more than one occasion in my life, usually after a heartbreak, I have quipped to friends that I should have gotten married to a cowboy and lived in a trailer. That is what I should have done. That is the answer given loud and clear by my culture. If he had been a preacher instead of a cowboy, I would have won the approval of my religious friends. Now, I know heartbreak is not the exclusive prerogative of "the homosexual." I know a cowboy and a trailer, or a preacher and church, would not have led to my happiness. Nevertheless I can't help wishing that life was that easy. That sexuality was that easy. But it isn't. And the responsibility of deluding men and women that it is – that it should be, that if it isn't there is something wrong with you, sinful in you – rests solidly on the shoulders of the Christian church. In the rural isolation of the Bible Belt this responsibility is in the hands of a few conservative preachers, followed by millions, devoted to imposing such illusory gender norms.

With all of this said, I return to Mr Brown, sitting in the twilight under his elm tree. It is true that when I close my eyes and conjure a picture of the Southern man, it is Mr Brown that comes clearly into focus. He is the romantic cowboy, the loving father, the working-class hero. His image is as comforting as a Texas sunset. But it is a childhood memory glorified by the passage of time. I wish I could have really known him, for the stories here highlight the discrepancy between image and reality. In this particular social context the normative image of manhood is impossible to achieve. Reality for these men is nothing more than frustrated attempts at "manhood," accompanied by the need to blame and to regain power. While this chapter has touched upon the difficulties of becoming a "man" in the South, the following chapters testify that it is absolute hell to be anything else.

NOTES

1 M. Kimmel and M. Messner, *Men's Lives* 2nd edn (New York: Macmillan, 1992). For further discussion concerning masculinity, see H. Brod (ed.), *The Making of Masculinities* (Boston: Unwin, Hyman, 1987); R. W. Connell, *Gender and Power* (Stanford, CA: Stanford University Press, 1987); R. W. Connell, *Masculinities* (Cambridge: Polity, 1995); G. Gilder, *Men and Marriage* (Gretna, LA: Pelican Publishers, 1986); S. Goldberg, *The Inevitability of Patriarchy* (New York: William Morrow & Co., 1975); J. Hearn, *The Gender of Oppression* (New York: St. Martin's Press, 1987); R. Wilkinson, *American Tough: The Tough Guy Tradition and American Character* (New York: Harper & Row, 1986).

2 M. Kimmel and M. Messner, *Men's Lives*, p. 18.

3 *Ibid.*, p. 97.

4 M. Kimmel (ed.), *Changing Men* (London, Sage, 1987), p. 238.

5 *Ibid.*

6 D. Minkowitz, "In the Name of the Father," *Ms. Magazine* (New York, November/December, 1995), pp. 64–71.

7 *Ibid.*, p. 67.

Chapter Three

ONE IS NOT BORN A LADY

Wives, be subject to your husbands, as to the Lord.   (Ephesians 5:22)

*A good wife who can find? ... Strength and dignity are her clothing,
and she laughs at the time to come.*   (Proverbs 31:10, 25)

Once upon a time I wanted to be a girl. In the twilight of my
tomboy days, my dad was appointed to a new church and I looked
forward to all the possibilities of a new school and new friends.
Unfortunately, and for any number of reasons – I was the preacher's daughter; my good grades and basketball talent upset the
teenage social order; my bad hair, braces, irritating contact lenses
constantly scratching my eyes making me an "ugly squint-eyed
horror" – my classmates decided to make my life hell. The 12
months our family endured in that God-forsaken town were quite
significant to my development, even in some positive ways. For
example, I learned to be fairly independent and eventually acquired
a decent amount of self-confidence. Self-doubt was a luxury I could
not afford. Nevertheless, those qualities are the result of time spent
"processing" rather than a gift of support handed to me by anyone
within a 40-mile radius of our front door. The immediate effect of
this total exclusion was my determination not to let it happen
again. So by the time we moved the following summer, my hair was
styled, the braces off, the contact lenses comfortable and the social
lessons learned. Whatever it took, I was going to be popular.

We arrived at the new parsonage on Wednesday morning.
Wednesday evening three boys were on the doorstep. I knew I was
on the right track when the cheerleaders began offering me a lift to
school. After a few weeks they sat me down and extended true
friendship – on one condition: if I was to be their friend, I had to get

laid. Fortunately, one of their older brothers had volunteered to do the job. On the appointed night the excitement was too much – for him. He never told that I didn't do "it"; I never told that he had finished "it" before I unzipped my jeans. That was my only attempt in high school to meet the requirements of my gender. Eventually, in college, I realized that I didn't have to.

Nevertheless I am always painfully aware that I *should* have grown up to be a lady. I am not the only one. Texan political humorist, Molly Ivins, writes about her own inability to meet gender requirements:

> I've always been more of an observer than a participant in Texas Womanhood: the spirit was willing but I was declared ineligible on grounds of size early. You can't be six feet tall and cute, both. I think I was first named captain of the basketball team when I was four and that's what I've been ever since. I spent my girlhood as a Clydesdale among thoroughbreds. I clopped along amongst them cheerfully, admiring their grace, but the strange training rituals they went through left me secretly relieved that no one would ever expect me to step on a racetrack. I think it is quite possible to grow up in Texas as an utter failure in flirting, gentility, cheerleading, sexpottery, and manipulation and still be without any permanent scars. Except one. We'd all rather be blonde.[1]

Personally, I don't know what she has to complain about: at four feet eleven inches I could only dream of being basketball captain. However, there is a sense in which every Southern woman knows what she should be. And in the Bible Belt what she should be is defined by Southern genteel patriarchy, and his best friend Christianity. "Eve was made from Adam," I have often been told, "not the other way around." A Christian lady is to be subservient to men. If she is not tied to one particular man, then at least she should be deferential to the sons of patriarchy. Such homage requires a woman to offer her very self as a sacrifice – her dreams, her profession and, most of all, her sexuality. In a culture where good Christian ladies should only bother themselves with family, home, and church, women struggle to make for themselves any socially acceptable space.

Of course there are benefits to clarity of gender expectations. There are a few times when even I, heart-broken, lonely, and miserable, have wished that I had simply married a man. A legally bound partner, whose income was half mine, can look seductively secure. And all I would have to do is cook a few meals and keep the house tidy. Then I remember the sex and come to my senses. But for heterosexual women, I assume that could be a bonus rather than a deterrent. The security of marriage and family, according to popular culture, can be obtained rather easily – the right make-up provided by Mary Kay or (depending on wallet size), perhaps Wal-Mart. Look the part and get the man. Cheerleaders and beauty queens in every small town know how to do it. They all seem to be striving to be the perfect looking lady. Hell, even Hillary Clinton, that icon of tough Southern womanhood, had a makeover and published her cookie recipe during her husband's campaign.

On the other hand, maybe Hillary is striving for something else. Her plight is that of one who knows what image she must portray in order to create space for her own desires. It is the constant struggle of most married working women – to be everything: perfect wife, mother, lover, cleaner, cook, *and* have a self-realized life and career. Perhaps unsurprisingly, it is that struggle that connects the women in this chapter. They are striving to be Southern ladies, and a little bit more. Each woman attempts this in her own way. Some compartmentalize the home, where Christianity says the man is king and patriarchy says he shouldn't do the dishes – separating it from her life outside the home where she gets fulfillment through her career. Those unable to do this, we will discover, sacrifice a bit of themselves on the altar of social acceptance.

Historically there are two images of Southern womanhood which are worth noting here.[2] To a large extent these can be identified along lines of class. The "Southern belle" is of course the middle-class white woman, who, as Molly Ivins testifies, we all should be. I have selected a few of these voices in the section below. While it is important to acknowledge these ladies, it is perhaps more interesting to hear the way in which they embrace social stratification. The other image is that of the "farm wife," or non-elite white woman. If one can't be a lady, one can be proud of her toughness during hard times. The second section considers the stories of three such women. While they struggle to be all that Southern culture requires of them, they also struggle with the knowledge that either they do not want to be, or they have no hope of ever becoming, a lady.

All of the women in this chapter have two other aspects in common. They are all white. The silence of Black voices in this chapter affirms the methodological difficulties in this research. I approached over a dozen Black women, all of whom viewed me with suspicion – even more so when I explained what the research was about. A couple agreed to chat with me but were unable to do so: one canceled because she was called into work; the other because her boss "discouraged" her. But the silence here is due to more than just my random methodology. Most significantly, it testifies to the continuing gulf between Black and white in the South and to the few bridges across that divide. And to the stories of Southern Black women living in small rural towns that need to be told. Unsurprisingly, racism finds its voice below.

In addition, not one of the women described herself as a lesbian. I do not know if they are all heterosexual. I think most are. At least one shared, off the record, that she has struggled with her sexual identity but has now "on God's direction" turned against "that way of life." Her decision to live as a straight woman itself tells us a lot about the intensity of Bible Belt expectations of gender. In turn each story affirms the struggle of becoming a Southern lady and, in some, of the despair.

LADIES, LADIES

As noted, images of rural Southern white women have emerged primarily from two historical characterizations: the Southern belle and the farm wife. The legacy of the non-elite white women we will consider in the next section. First I want to briefly consider the historical construction of the Southern belle. Through the years,

Hollywood has provided us with an image of the genteel magnolia, complete with frills and lace, sipping mint juleps on the porch of the plantation house, thinking only of the next ball. She can also be just a little feisty. The mythical Scarlett O'Hara epitomized the tempestuous Southern belle. As historian Nina Silber notes, it was in fact Northerners who engendered this image during the Civil War:

> When the Civil war began, Confederate propaganda assigned women a role that was anything but tempestuous. Urged to send men willingly, even cheerfully, off to war, white southern women were then expected to wait silently and patiently at home, finding appropriate and refined ways to boost army morale. Given southern society's conception of women's patriarchal subservience to men, Confederate literature generally did not allow for a more active and aggressive part for its females. But in light of the fact that southern women would often find themselves in direct contact with enemy troops (much more so than northern women), the frustration of being part of the fight but circumscribed in their actions undoubtedly intensified the wartime anguish of Confederate ladies ... This sense of frustration seems to have played a significant part in pushing some southern women into a role that northerners would later see as typical of all southern womanhood. Unable to respond with force, some women, especially those in Union-occupied areas, turned to whatever means they had at their disposal to show their opposition to the Union army – their skirts, their words, their manner of walking, their handkerchiefs, even their chamberpots. In this way, some southern females managed to make a fine art out of rudeness and insolence ... Because of her assumed aristocratic inclinations (and perhaps also because southern white women were rarely found in positions of paid labor), the southern white woman could serve as a symbol of northern reform goals, especially the desire to instill in the white South an appreciation for good, old-fashioned work.[3]

Since this creation, the Southern belle has been known for her self-appointed nobility and, when threatened, her "fine art" of rudeness and insolence. And in the post-Civil War South this myth became a normative identity romanticized by white middle-class women. She became a heroic image of one who fights her battles, protecting her investment in the social order, while always conducting herself as a lady.

Representations of this Southern lady can be located in contemporary urban culture from *Dallas* to *Good and Evil* Savannah. She is the wealthy wife who does not work for pay but volunteers for all the right charities; she is the hostess whose parties include only the right people; she is the beauty queen, whose layers of make-up, "big hair" and plastic surgery defy mother nature. In a culture where class is confused with wealth, this urban lady lives off "Daddy's money" – either through marriage or divorce.

Similarly, her rural cousin relies upon the family name and assumed wealth. In her rural isolation she may be forced to define wealth less extensively but her husband's name establishes her place in the community as an old family, an insider, sufficiently distinguishing her from "others" – outsiders or tolerated undesirables. Sometimes with Confederate vengeance, the rural lady protects her territory by organizing "civil" activities and by ensuring the exclusion of those who do not meet communal standards. She may even acquire some sort of paid employment. Depending on the woman, and the extenuating circumstances, this may mean starting a small business such as a restaurant or clothes boutique, or it may simply mean selling cosmetics or insurance "on the side." This serves a two-fold purpose of adding to the family income – "keeping the wife busy" – and increasing her social/political placement within the community. However, while she struggles to meet gendered expectations and have a career, she rarely questions oppressive social structures. Using whatever means at her disposal, the Southern lady is keen to ensure the continuance of a social order which offers some power over the working-class white or Black "other."

Somewhere along the Tennessee/Mississippi border, my stomach reminded me that breakfast had been hours before and had consisted of only coffee and sunflower seeds. Just as I stuffed another handful in my mouth I caught sight of a billboard advertising "Harlan's Cafe." My trip so far had felt like a solo *Thelma and Louise*, so I had to stop. Thinking that any encounter with Harlan may necessitate firearms, I was pleasantly surprised to find that the owner of this fine establishment was a woman. As I polished off a rather large plate of Southern Fried Chicken and complementary peach cobbler, I inquired if she would be willing to have a quick cup of coffee with me and "visit." Linda kindly agreed and for the next couple of hours told me all about the nice folks of "Podunk." Her husband's family were amongst the original settlers in the area and most of the family still lived there. There were "five, maybe six old families" that were the "core" of the community. They rarely moved away and so had an investment in making the place a "good little town." Given this, and her own interests as a business-woman active in various civic clubs and charities, she of course told me the best stuff first:

The population is 4,039 people, but there is more than that in the county, almost 15,000. This small town is personal. In the big city you're anonymous, people don't know you, you don't know them, even your neighbors. You may see them but you don't necessarily know them. In a small community everybody is depending upon everybody. Everybody who lives on your street, you know where they work and you know what they do. Even if you are not their best friend you're connected to them somehow because everything here is supported by each person. Like if you shop here that helps the businesses here. If you raise your children here and send them to school here, then you are involved with the people whether they live right next door to you or across town. It's still all the same small community where you are responsible either directly or indirectly for each other ... We just have to help each other ... everybody is responsible for everybody else because if you are not successful and they are not successful, nobody is ... you have to watch out for each other. It's a good town. There is a lot of church stuff. There's like 13 churches here ... the people are real conservative ... real "family values," not liberal at all, in any way. Very family values.

There are a lot of service organizations here: Rotary Clubs; there are three Lions Clubs – Men's Breakfast and Men's Lunch and then a Women's Lunch; and then [there] are Optimists Clubs; Boy Scouts, Girl Scouts. You name it, we've got it ... We ladies always had our own separate organization – the Lady Lions. There is now no designation, a man could join a women's club, a woman could join a men's club. But just out of courtesy, or whatever, the men stick in the men's clubs and the women stick in the women's clubs. Men were basically responsible for all the fundraising and everything, and now that there are women involved [through a separate club] it has taken on a different tone. Women are workers, as far as community service. Whenever you have women in a [men's or mixed] club they seem to get some of the less appealing jobs and even though it's not that they do it on purpose, but women just take on hard jobs that men won't handle. The men want to do the easy fundraising – I'll just give you a hundred bucks and don't make me work for it. But women, they do all kinds of stuff to raise money and they don't care how hard they have to work at it as long as it's fun and entertaining, like a bake sale, and everybody bakes and purchases cakes. But men aren't like that.

You see them like that in the Chamber [of Commerce]. Before when it was mostly men, the Chamber wasn't really active in fundraising and that kind of stuff. But when you get women in there, they go out, do their fundraising and do the hard work and everything. [She was recently the president of the Chamber of Commerce and since then] we have integrated more women onto the Board. There are more women who own businesses. There are more women who are involved in community affairs because it's important. The things that we do now affect our children now and later. If we don't try to make positive changes in our community today, our children will not be able to get good jobs when they grow up and be able to stay here – they will have to leave.

I go to the school, I volunteer, I do stuff with the teacher, like to help with the class. Parents who go to the school and participate are also better about participating in the home, reading to their children, spending time with them rather than sending them to the TV room and letting them do whatever ... They have a lot of programs to keep the kids involved. One for pregnant teenage mothers. They can go to school whilst they are pregnant, once the baby is born they have a day-care center that they take them to, so the mother will stay in school. It's a great program.

What? Teenage pregnancy in this ideal little rural conservative family values neighborly community? Containing my astonishment,

or lack of it, I asked her to tell me more about the troubles facing
girls in "Podunk." Her answer was not unlike many good Christian
women I have talked with about unwanted pregnancies, who are
concerned about teenage pregnancy ruining two young lives:

Twenty-four out of about 500 junior high students [14–15 years of
age] were pregnant at the beginning of the school year this year. It's
pathetic. They teach sex education ... But these kids are just bored.
They go to the dance. They have a little bit of alcohol. They get
pregnant. I think that is pretty standard nowadays. Most of them
have the baby. Personally I do not recommend that – especially to
a child of 14 or 15 years old. They don't need to be having babies
at that age. My personal opinion is that they should not be having
kids. But because of their religious beliefs or their families' beliefs,
they think it's better to have the baby. I don't agree with that. They
would have to drive 70 miles to get an abortion, and the parents
would have to be involved basically. I have two daughters who are
only six and four right now, but I am thinking that in ten years or
so I am going to be worried about this. So it does bother me. My
husband and I don't agree on how we would handle it. I don't
think a child should be having a baby. It's not fair to the child who
is pregnant and it's not fair to the baby who is not even born yet. If
a 14 or 15 year old child has a baby, who is responsible for that
baby?

Lulled into believing I had met a kindred spirit, I asked Linda about
other social difficulties facing the community. She hesitantly
acknowledged gangs in the school, alcohol and drug abuse and
then, ever so quickly, moved on to pinpoint the culprits. Scratch the
surface long enough in the South and the familiar beast will be
lurking underneath:

The worse thing that happens around here is that young kids start
messing around with alcohol. But no ... the worse thing is drugs in
our community. It's everywhere, you just can't say it doesn't exist,
because it does. And they say that there is gang activities at the
school. Marijuana, crack cocaine ... There has been a couple of
shootings over in the dark side of town. Our town is divided by a

railroad track and a main highway into like four squadrons; black, white, white, black – the colored side of town, the black side of town. It is very segregated and that's unfortunate. But that's the way it is, and it has always been that way. Everybody who is Black lives in one side of town and they don't live anywhere else – unless they live in the low income housing apartment complexes which are in some other areas. [The town is] probably about 25 percent Black, 25 percent Hispanic and the rest white.

The Black women basically do the domestic kind of work – work in the school, in the cafeterias, or here, like in the restaurant, some work in the grocery stores, checking groceries, or whatever. The men do a variety of things – we have had quite a few go to college on sports scholarships. I think a lot of the Black men when they grow up want to get out of town and don't come back. The ones who are here are older. They either work in the farming communities, driving a tractor or whatever.

In this community your clubs are basically Anglo-American. They are not real mixed up. There is not a lot of Black people. There is probably more Hispanics involved but there is hardly any Black people involved in the community clubs and such. Of course there is not many Black businessmen. And this being basically largely a German community, these people are real funny about that kind of stuff. I mean ten years ago Black people still went in the back doors of a lot of businesses. They didn't go through the front doors. They were on a different level than everybody else. In small town USA, unless it's predominantly Black, predominantly Mexican, predominantly white, you don't really see how separate things are until you are in a town where it is very divided by a railroad track. It's very apparent.

Driving through the leafy countryside the little town had indeed looked idealistic. Church steeples, and nicely kept homes lined the main road. However, as Linda herself admitted, look closely and one gets a different picture. Alcohol and drug abuse and teenage pregnancy make "Podunk" just like any other American town. A railroad track dividing its citizens by color makes it like any other Southern town. Linda's concern for local prosperity extends only to white families, so it is little wonder that the young Black men want to leave, and little wonder why the remaining Black women find it hard to find jobs beyond the "domestic."

Linda does seem to struggle with the position of (white) women to the extent that civic interactions with men seem almost subversive. When ladies do most of the work, they can gradually gain some power. Although it appears that this power is limited most in their own home. Having noted that she and her husband held different views on abortion, Linda was unwilling to explore their differences of opinion any further. Ladies do not discuss their dirty laundry, or family conflicts, in public. And while I am sure a lady of her stature would belong to a church, she wouldn't speak about her personal faith. Perhaps it was another club, perhaps it was deeply personal, perhaps its teachings contradicted her desired position in the community. She reminded me of a few church members I knew growing up – business women, intelligent, assertive, leaders in the community who every Sunday would tacitly take their place beside their husband in the pew reading Paul's message about subservience in marriage. Apparently such ladies are comfortable with these contradictions and are unable, or unwilling, to see any similarities between their struggle with the gendered social order and struggles with classism or racism.

Northwest of Atlanta, near Newt Gingrich[4] country, I came across a woman who explained the situation to me. I had stopped off at a pretty little Baptist church in hopes of talking with the pastor. He was busy but suggested I interview his secretary, an elderly woman who had lived all of her life in the small town. Alma made me a cup of coffee and we settled into the rather comfortable surroundings of an adult Sunday school room. She had been born and raised in the house she still lived in and her daughter's family lived just down the road. Her husband, Ray, was a "retired" farmer, but spent every day working at the farm. She volunteered three days a week at the church typing up the newsletter, sending out birthday cards to members and generally "keeping the pastor in line." We talked a bit about her family and her work at the church. "My son lives in Atlanta but gets home every once in a while for a visit. My daughter's husband is a farmer and she is a teacher at the elementary school. My husband and I are really proud of them ... Of course I didn't work while the kids were home. I have always done various volunteer things. But that's not really work, that's the Lord's work."[5] Alma seemed proud of her kids, but a bit concerned about the amount of time her daughter spent at work, away from her duties at home. When I asked about this she confided:

Yes, well, she has a busy life and well, sometimes that don't always make a good wife. A wife's first duty is to her husband and kids ... meeting their needs. Ray didn't want me working outside the home. He had to be up early and needed a good breakfast and a solid meal when he got home. And of course the kids needed picking up after school and they had school activities. I needed to be there for them. Now that they are grown, I tend to other people's needs. That's what the Lord has told me to do ... Ray has been a deacon here most of our married life. Our marriage has been based on Christ's example. You know what the Bible says about marriage? The man is the head of the household and his wife should be subject to him, just as we are subject to Christ. Do you know Proverbs 12:4? "A good wife is the crown of her husband." That means a good wife makes her husband king, and then he can be a good man ... Of course, Joyce [her daughter] belongs to this church too. Her and her husband grew up in this church. And when they got married, we talked with them about what had made us last so long. Joyce believes, like me, that her place is always beside her husband, tending to his needs ... well, what with that and teaching, and the two kids, she is very busy. Sometimes I have to remind her what her priorities should be. She likes having fine things and wants the children to have the latest fashion. So she works. And her husband works hard. Sometimes, well, sometimes I think she gets a bit too worried about things in the community, you know, this club, that school activity, looking a certain way, and well, forgets who the Lord says should be wearing the pants. But I am sure she realizes how important it is. Just last weekend she attended a women's retreat. Her husband is a Promise Keeper. You know? And this retreat was organized by the church for women whose husbands are Promise Keepers. The pastor spoke quite plainly ... reminding them of their duties. Joyce was very moved. I think it will make a change.

I asked if she thought it would be possible to chat with her daughter and Alma gladly arranged for me to meet with Joyce after school. So late afternoon I found my way through the corridors to a sixth-grade classroom. Joyce had only 30 minutes so I jumped straight in with a few questions about her religious beliefs and marriage. She explained that she had felt difficulties juggling her responsibilities, but after the spiritual retreat had "offered them to the Lord" and no longer experienced stress. She had duties to fulfill and rather than worrying about the future she simply "left that to God." Now she gets through each day with her priorities set by the Lord – "my husband, my children, and service of the Lord." Having tired slightly of hearing this version of "service," I asked her about her job, her needs. "Teaching is stressful, of course. And we don't really need the money. But as long as I am meeting the needs of my husband ... and of course I am at school where my children are all day." I asked again about her needs and personal goals. And was assured that her goal was to be a "good servant of the Lord and everything else will be taken care of." I tried again, asking her about her job fulfillment. Her students were mostly "good kids from good homes."

> But we have some difficult kids ... mostly the Blacks who start fights and don't try at school ... There are a couple of white kids from the government apartments who are a bit of a problem ... but I think they don't get support at home ... mostly it's the Black kids who have no father, mothers who work all hours, and just get into things they shouldn't ... Each year I get a few of them. Not many. There are only a handful that live here. I don't think they like it here. It's a lovely town, but I guess you get those type anywhere. God help me if I taught in Atlanta. Well, I just couldn't do it.

I left the school feeling like I had known Joyce for years. Or at least a hundred like her – white, middle-class, Christian women whose ideas of mission, or service, are confined to family and good (white) local citizens. The troubles of the world are too overwhelming, too far away, and too easy to solve with a tithe. Social problems in their town? "Well," they would respond, "that's just their own fault and nothing to do with me."

These ladies speak of their work and their place in the community as important to them, while simultaneously they either remain silent or proudly acknowledge their subservience to their husbands. What appears confusing, if not contradictory, to me seems simply the natural order to them. Likewise what appears to me as their struggle to be a Southern lady of the 1990s, to them is simply their "calling," what defines them as good Christian ladies. The Lord's needs, and their husbands', are trump cards shuffling their own needs to the side.

Feminism, unsurprisingly, has a rather limited history in the South. In her enlightening piece, "Second Wave Feminism(s) and the South," Jane Sherron De Hart highlights the number of women who were against ratification of the Equal Rights Amendment.[6] She notes one woman who wrote to her senator: "My husband works for me and takes care of me and our three children, doesn't make me do things that are hard for me (drive in town), loves me and doesn't smoke, drink, gamble, run around or do anything that would upset me. I do what he tells me to do. I like this arrangement. *It's the only way I know how to live.*"[7] Another woman wrote: "*Forced* busing, *forced* mixing, *forced* housing. Now *forced* women! No thank you!"[8] LeeAnn Whites notes that in the post-Civil War South women honored their men by waiving their citizenship rights. For example, one women's organization wrote, "Southern ladies naturally shrink from contact with the outside world."[9] She also draws our attention to historians who acknowledge that women were central to the Klu Klux Klan: "Ex-Confederate women designed and made more than four hundred thousand Klan robes for both rider and horse ... [which were to] symbolize the central aim of the Klan, the 'purity and preservation of the home'."[10] The patriarchy of the Confederacy, combined with compulsory Christianity of the Bible Belt, yoke women with a concept of service and of gender inferiority. Any attempts to remove it by an outsider meet God's wrath executed by both Southern gentlemen and Southern ladies. As the stories below testify, attempts to remove it by individual Southern women like-wise meet with severe disapproval.

BECOMING A WOMAN

In "The Ideal Woman in the Ante-bellum South: Lady or Farm-wife?" Harland Hagler points out that the mythology of the South-ern belle obscures the fact that the majority of white women were living in poverty.[11] Most worked either as domestic servants – with the same social position as a slave – or were at the mercy of religion or of well-meaning ladies. Similarly, Timothy Lockley tells of their "Struggle for Survival" in a world which kept them in domestic service, controlled them in charitable institutions, or encouraged them to marry.[12] The only other option was prostitution in urban centers providing a small income by, of course, servicing men. In rural areas, her options were usually limited to that of farmwife. It is this farmwife, or rural working-class woman, which resonates with the stories below. As it is the image that haunts my own life, I know it is not an easy one to live up to. A farmwife can plow the fields, tend the herd, chop the wood, shoot any target, all while giving birth, raising kids, cleaning the house, feeding the family, and nursing through illness every friend and neighbor. And on Saturday night, she "cleaned up nice enough" for her man to take her to the nearest barn dance. In other words, she is a pretty damn good wife, but she sure as hell ain't no lady.

The gender requirements of this contemporary, non-elite white woman are slightly different than that of a lady. She must work hard, stand by her man, and always know her place – in particular, the difference between herself and a lady. Despite her hardships, or perhaps because of them, she maintains a strong sense of pride. In Texas, such women are often called "kicker women" (referring to their boots or "shitkickers"). Molly Ivins comments upon their well-earned pride, advising never to ask what a kicker kicks. The kicker equivalent of wealth starts as, "Every Texas girl's dream is a double-wide [trailer] in a Lubbock trailer park." Ivins continues,

But I personally believe it is unwise ever to be funny at the expense of kicker women. I once met a kicker lady who was wearing a blouse of such a vivid pink you could close your eyes and still see the color; this confection was perked up with some big rhinestone buttons and a lot of ruffles across an impressive bosom. "My," said I, "where did you get that blouse?" She gave me a level look and drawled, "Honey, it come from mah coutouri-ay, Jay Cee Penn-ay." And if that ain't class, you can kiss my grits (UK read ASD-ay).[13]

This classy kicker woman is a hard worker who, after raising a family and meeting her husband's demands, has little time for "civil" activities. She may have a night out every now and then, and will probably just make it to church on Sunday morning. If the family has lived in the town for a few generations, she will be relatively accepted, as part of the landscape. Her husband isn't a pillar of the community, or even economically active, but she will "stand by her man." In short, she is as tough as an old boot, but probably because she has trudged through a lot of shit. The sacrifices she has made should give her every right to participate fully in the community. But her economic positioning, and lack of education, keep her just out of reach of the category "lady."

With the possibility of being a Southern lady beyond her reach, the life of the working-class woman – farmwife, kicker lady – becomes one of struggle to negotiate her social marginalization. The stories below are each marked by the woman's uneasiness with her own difference. Each has struggled, consciously, to marry gender(ed) expectations with individual desires. And in each case, their public struggle has given way to a triumph of public gender norms. But such public acting out of gender norms has not led to private resignation. As the women speak about their lives we can see their internal conflict – signs of a continued sense of loss, of despair, and of rebellion.

Probably one story I most enjoyed hearing as a child was about my cousin Teri. She was a few years older than me, lived somewhere in East Texas, and was a cowgirl. But not just any cowgirl. Teri rode bulls. Now for those of you who have never spent a summer evening in the rickety stands surrounding a rodeo arena, watching cowboys exert their dominance over enormous untamed horses and bulls, or showing off their agility at ranch jobs such as roping and wrestling cattle, I lament your lack of culture. There is nothing better than dressing up in boots and jeans, drinking beer while the sun sets in the Texas sky, and pretending, if only for a few moments, that you too are a part of the wild west. The rules of the rodeo are far too complex for me to go into here, even if I knew them. But generally, cowboys do really amazing physical feats while the clock and judges scientifically calculate their "score." There is one rule that I do know for sure: as participants, cowgirls can either "barrel race" (a timed event where she displays her prolific horse-riding abilities by directing the animal around three barrels), or cowgirls can be rodeo queen contestants (not sure of the rules but I think it has something to do with how good they look in Levis). Cowgirls do not – I repeat do not – ride bulls. Except my cousin Teri. She was the best bull rider, ever. Or so the story goes. And as this family legend was such a vivid part of my childhood, when I began thinking about interviewing Southern women for this book, I had to hear her story:

My parents bought us [three sisters] horses when we were little. And we three sisters were all in to them at the time, but I am the only one that stuck with it. They both out grew of it. When I was at high school [age 14–18] there was a rodeo team, the girls did barrel racing. Well I didn't really get into barrel racing, I didn't want to do that. That was what the girls did, but I had to do what the guys did! So, that was how I got into bull riding. I just rode bulls. I had a horse but I didn't want to barrel race. I didn't want to barrel race and so I didn't fit in with the other girls that much. I was more tomboy and I wasn't into the frilly things.

The first time I rode was at Mount Pleasant. Papa [grandfather] entered me into an open rodeo. I was the only girl. Papa paid my entry fee and we all went up there that night. I didn't have a bull rope or spurs or nothing, I borrowed it all. The guys put me on there and said, "just stick your chest out, and your head down, and ride." And I did. Didn't even know that I was supposed to open my hand to release the rope so I hung up [caught on the bull]. The clown got me off. I didn't get stepped on, I was too small. I knew then that I wanted to keep on doing it. It just gives you that thrill.

My parents thought probably one time would be enough. I was only 13, 14. And Dad, he was real proud, he always went and pulled my rope for me on the bull. I was trying to impress Dad. That was part of the reason I started it.

After joining the rodeo team at school, Teri's parents began to get concerned about the physical danger. And she began to get signs of the social dangers:

Well, I rode for a couple of years. Then a boy was killed in the finals in my third year, so I couldn't get on the rodeo team. Mother told me I couldn't ride no more. So I didn't get on the team but I did sneak around and ride and I didn't tell her. And I'd go to practices and stuff like that. There was one other girl – she got hurt. She was really skinny and a bit frail. But she never did really get into it like I did. She was barrel racing too so that was really more her thing.

Other girls doing barrel racing couldn't believe I was doing it. But then, you know, they stopped saying stuff after a while, you know, after I could ride and they knew that I could do it. I had a good friend that did barrel racing and she never did say anything.

I had a boyfriend and he didn't like it. When I first rode, the very first time I rode in the high school rodeo, I still wasn't sure what I was going on. I had practiced, and I just about rode him [the bull]. The second time I went on I just about rode him but then he turned back and came up the fence. I fell between the fence and him, and he kind of smashed me and dragged me ... he didn't hurt me but he scratched my face so I had lines down my face. And he [the boyfriend] didn't like it at all. He couldn't believe I was doing it. He started making fun of me. He called me "Miss Bullrider," "Miss Toughie." He wasn't handling it too well. He was probably jealous or something. He came and saw me a couple of times but that was it. And I rode every weekend so there was a lot of weekends but he only came a couple of times. He would pretty much make fun of me.

Teri enjoyed the ride as much as she enjoyed proving herself to the cowboys. She recalls once when she attended a rodeo and decided when she got there to enter and ride:

Two guys were riding bulls and I went up and I asked them if I could ride, just for fun. They said OK, and made me sign a release form. This guy that I was talking to, he was one of the ones that was riding and he got bucked off, and I said "I'll ride that one right there!" [The bull that had just bucked him off.] And I rode him all the way up [rode the bull for the required eight seconds]. Neither one of the guys could ride that bull. Oh they were embarrassed. They didn't say anything.

The other time that I did that to this man ... we were at this prac-tice and I walked up there, and said I was going to ride and this man said, "Will you need to borrow a bull rope?" and I said, "No I've got it." "You need a glove or anything?" I said, "No, I've got it." And he said "Do you need spurs?" and I said, "No thanks, I've brought everything I need." And then I kind of did what I did to the other fella. I saw him get bucked off this bull and I told them that was the one I wanted. And I rode him and the fella never said another word to me. I just think they can't deal with it.

The family legend had not been a fairy tale. She could do it just as good as any man. But sitting before me was a pretty strong looking young woman, why had she stopped? There are professional women's rodeos now where women participate in every event, I had seen them on TV. At what point had she stopped doing something she loved and was obviously great at? The answer is as unsurprising as it is sad:

Then after I got married, which was probably six years ago, was the last time I rode ... When I joined the high school team they had bulls for women. But now they don't even have that for girls in high school. They do have women's professional rodeo association and they have got bulls and bare back and stuff. They just had the finals last weekend, near here. I was inspired. I knew that I could do it [ride professional] because I saw what they were riding, you know. The ones that covered the bulls [rode successfully] were a little dinks. I know what my abilities were ... in my mind I still could do it. If I got in shape. Really I can't think of any bad wrecks. I was pretty much like a cat back then, I could land on my feet. I mean I was really aware of where the bull was. I never had any close calls. I never can remember getting hung up after that very first time. I mean, I know it's rough, but I feel I could do it. Because those women are older than I am, some of them were – they were gray headed. But the rodeos for women are just not like for men's – they don't pay as well and they are really far apart so you have to drive so far and it's just ... not like the men's yet. Maybe it will be some day. But it's just a neat thrill, which you can't imagine.

I now have a son, you know, I've got to think about him ... I would be kind of scared to ... I get nervous just watching it on TV. I feel like I'm on the bull and I start jerking, and I can't stand to see a bad wreck, you know, somebody getting hung up and getting hurt ... it's just ... If he wasn't here, I know without a doubt I know I would do it, I know. I think that's why I am team roping, because I'm in the competition part of it at least, and I can do it until I'm old.

It is at least worth noting that Teri stopped bull riding when she got married. Now that she is a mom, she has to think about her responsibility and desire to stay healthy. She enjoys being a mom and is proud of her little man. Reflecting upon her own life and expectations for her kids, Teri is concerned about their safety but also open to their need to fulfill their own desires:

I want him to hopefully rope and stay with that kind of stuff – bull dog or rope or something safer ... A daughter would definitely be a horse person and ride a horse. But I might want her to stay with the timed events, like the barrel racing. If she wanted to ride bulls it would be tough, but if she really had the desire, I would let her do it.

In my mind, Teri remains a legend. But like any legend, she too lives in the real world. A world which will allow a girl to have dreams beyond her "natural" gender, as long as in womanhood she "sets aside her childish ways." Teri is not that much older than me, perhaps this is why her story caught my childish imagination. And why I see her spark of rebellion – she remains a strong woman, and has yet to give in to the "big hair brigade" – lighting up the corners of her heart that continue to lament the impact of gender socialization. She is not the only one.

Somewhere in Kentucky, I found a little farm owned by a "friend of a friend of a friend" – an "interesting" older woman who had once been a university lecturer and had returned to the homeplace to live in isolation. My contact had shared with me only a few background details. Louise grew up on a family farm, an only child. She had been an excellent basketball player just when women were beginning to be allowed to play the sport. Her parents, not fond of education, had allowed her to attend college but refused, or were unable, to pay for it. She eventually finished a masters degree and began teaching history at a small liberal arts college in the 1960s. She only taught for a couple of years when, without warning, returned to her parents' farm. She never married and since her parents' death continues to live on the farm, keeping to herself. It was questionable if she would even speak with me. I rang, sent letters, and upon arrival in the nearby small town held my breath while I dialed her number. She remembered me and eventually agreed to tell me the way through the maze of backroads to her house. As it turned out, her isolation was not chosen but somewhat imposed. We spent a number of hours talking about her childhood, life at college, brief teaching career, and her disappointments. While I have attempted to place her story in chronological order for simplicity, I have chosen to leave large sections uninterrupted by my commentary:

> I caught the school bus about 7 o'clock in the morning and got in about 5, and as soon as I got in I went and either made myself get on a horse and go get the milk cows, or walked. I preferred walking. I don't like horses. And then we milked about 14 cows every morning and every night – by hand, we didn't know anything else. I was in the second grade before we ever got electricity. You ain't done nothing yet until you've got that deadgum number three wash tub, and then we ironed our sheets, underwear, pillow cases, cuptowels, everything. And we did it by heating those irons on the stove and then ironing with them.
>
> And my dad, he said that I had to graduate from high school but

he considered that to be "it." That's fine. He graduated from the fifth grade and then he quit because he knew more than the teachers did ... so that gives you an idea about my dad. But dad said that I should finish high school or I could keep going until I was 25. Whenever I graduated from high school, I didn't know what I was going to do. I assumed I was going to farm because I did not want business ... I mean being a secretary was the farthest thing from my mind. That was the most gross thing. And then I had an opportunity ... a coach asked "Would you like to play basketball and go to college?" Everybody was so encouraging about that ... I kept hearing, "Well, you might be there six weeks and you'll flunk out." I knew I couldn't play basketball much because I had damaged my knees and stuff. I was being taped from thighs down, and it was hurting so bad. But if I quit playing I'd have to go home because I didn't have the money to stay – Daddy said you can go to school as much as you want to but you've got to pay for it. So I got me a job – or two. Then of course every weekend I came home and farmed. My parents would come and pick me up and they would take me back Monday morning. And whenever I got through college, I didn't owe anybody anything.

I lived in the oldest dorm because it was the cheapest, and it had a balcony. Girls were not allowed to wear pants. So one night we were getting ready to go to supper and I wore this big full circle skirt, corduroy red circle skirt. And I bet those girls – the little nuts that didn't have any sense – that I could jump off that balcony. Well I'd jumped off enough hay stacks to know the distance, so I made a mad dash and jumped off. And the skirt just caught all the air in the world. I was like a big helium balloon coming down. But I won my bet.

You see whenever I went to college as a student, I had big time trouble – I *had* no dresses. I didn't even *own* a dress. And my mom made me some skirts and blouses and dresses to take to college ... Oh I lived at college. If you want to call that living. It was odd, it was unusual because ... I don't make friends. It's just as simple as that. I am a very definite loner. I do basically what I want to. I found out I could make friends at college and then all of a sudden I found it wasn't what it was hyped up to be ... like: "Could you help me do this?" which turned out to be "Would you do this for me." And I would think, "Do I want to do this to keep your friendship?" – No. So that went down the tubes. Also whenever you're working the jobs I did, you don't have a whole lot of time.

I came home every weekend and plowed and gathered cotton. Before I started to college, we had 14 cows we had to milk morning and night; we had pigs to slop; we had chickens to feed; we had calves to take care of. By the end of the first semester of my freshman year the cows had been sold, the pigs had been sold, and what have you, because mom and daddy couldn't take care of them. And I couldn't very well drive over here every day and do that stuff. So they saw the writing on the wall and got rid of all the livestock.

Apparently, one of the reasons Louise had agreed to speak with me was that I had grown up in a small town and was a university lecturer. And it was while talking about the joys of teaching that her eyes lit up most. She began teaching during the Vietnam War. She told me about her surprise at the political protest in what was a small college town in the middle of nowhere, and her matter-of-fact farm girl response to it. I moved on to ask her about racial tensions on the Southern, predominantly white, campus. While her stories are marked by racism, they also testify to her struggle with its irrational demonization of people based on physical difference. And her struggle to recognize discrimination and its impact on individual lives:

I had boys in my class who were student deferment kids, sitting beside boys who had just come back from Vietnam. One boy said, "What would you do if I laid down in front of your car in protest?" And I said, "I would probably run over you." I said, "You have the right to lay down, and I have the right to run over you!" So, I never did have any trouble at all. Not any. I think they thought I would run over them.

The first Black kid I ever taught, my first year of teaching [teacher training in a high school setting], was when the school was first integrated. We had two Black boys in school, and it wasn't as if they were totally crazy. But they were so far down the educational scale, it was pathetic. History – their facts of history were all Black, like Ely Whitney was Black, anybody of any magnitude was

Black. I really never did know how to handle it. But we were a little worried, whenever we first started teaching the Blacks. Years later, I spoke to one of the boys, and we were talking about school and how we didn't know what to think of him, and he said, "Oh I hated the school." I said, "You had us all faked out." He was voted "most wittiest," believe or not, by the student body. "Oh I hated you all," he said, "What did I have at the school? ... Nothing." He said, "If I wanted to go on a date, what do you think they would have done to me if I'd have asked one of these lily white ladies up here for a date?" I said, "They would have strung you up." He said, "You're right! Don't you think I wanted to have a date? When we went to school, we went home because we couldn't have any interaction with the kids. I kept myself straight and not in trouble by making everything funny." He said, "There were times when I just wanted to smash all of your white faces in." And I said, "I'm glad you didn't." I said, "Well, I really am so dumbfounded, well, I didn't realize it." So that was why ... but I didn't even give it a thought. I thought that those boys were wonderful young Black boys who were wonderfully hilarious, not too darn bright ... It was not that they weren't bright. I'm sorry. I shouldn't have said that. They were not educated. They were probably brighter than we were because they had to work doubly hard in order to try to catch up.

The only "encounter" I had with one Black college student was when he informed me he was Black and I wasn't. He was from Chicago, and he came down the aisle late at the lecture, which was a "no-no" for me anyway. He was already on my "black list," I guess you'd call it, because he was late. Secondly – and I was still the old farmer person – he had his hat on. Now you don't have your hat on in the house, in the presence of others. And I said, "Would you please remove your hat." He did – wrong thing to have done. He had the Afro. I mean, all this hair went out like this, and I thought, "How do I tell him to put it back on?" Well, during the discussion that day, on several occasions he made some excellent, excellent points, but he had to refer to the white kids as "honkies" in order to do it. As we were getting ready to leave I asked him to please meet me at my office. Now my office was about the size of a small bathroom. I mean, it had a desk, and you had to crawl over the desk to get to the chair. And he was at college on a basketball scholarship, so you know I'm talking a fairly good sized man. He walked into my office, and I walked in behind him and shut the door. "Well," I said, "Do you know why I would like to talk to you?" And he said, "Probably because I kept calling that honky a honky." And I said, "And yes, if it doesn't stop, I'm going to start calling you nigger." I said, "Does that sound good?" I said, "Let's make a deal right here." I said, "You don't call me a honky, and I won't call you a nigger, and we'll shake hands on it, and we'll enjoy our class for the rest of the year." So we shook hands, and afterwards he became a history major and I just thoroughly enjoyed teaching him. But I got to thinking, when he left, that I didn't have a chance against him in that office. He could have beat me to death. But he was a good kid, and he just had to try to show how macho he was, or something like that. I find that men, Black people, are a lot harder to deal with than the women are. I worked with some of the women over there at the women's center, and some of them were Black and the only thing they wanted to do was beat on their kids.

The Black people who lived in the area were treated badly. They were rotten egged, and some pretty serious things. Although they lived here, they went to school in the next town which had a Black school. Doesn't mean we were going to school together, no, no, no. That was not done. In '54 Brown versus Topeka Board of Education [stated that Southern schools were to be integrated "with all deliberate speed"]. Well, "all deliberate speed" was a long time in coming here. In 1962 they decided to integrate the school from the top down. You see they didn't start all the school at once. Just enough to keep from breaking the law.

I didn't go to school with any Black people until I was at college. And the first person I met there was Florence. She was from Nigeria. That was when Nigeria was getting their independence, and she was thrilled to bits. She was 25 years old and had been in the Olympics on the British team. She was very good. Her boyfriend was going to Harvard and they got married. I went to their wedding – which is one of the few weddings I ever went to in my life. But it was odd the way some people in the small college town treated the Black people at college. If they were from Nigeria or the Congo, oh they were welcomed into the [white] church. If they were from America, forget it, find yourself a Black church.

Stories of her own growing awareness of discrimination took a personal turn when I inquired as to why she had given up her teaching career. The power of labeling, the social demonization of difference touched her own life, bringing a promising career to an abrupt end:

By the time I was 35, in 1975, my career as a teacher ended. I was sick. And the illness that I had wasn't ever going to kill me, but it destroyed the fact that I wanted to teach. I am a diagnosed manic depressive. And when diagnosed the psychiatrist told me, "You do know your career as a teacher has ended?" And I said, "But I can still teach." He said, "But whenever you tell anybody they won't want you around their kids. They don't want you around anything. You are a pariah. You need to go somewhere and sit in a corner and do crossword puzzles. You can only go so long without them finding out. It does not matter how good you are, and how good a job you are doing, when they find out." So whenever that happened, I came home. And farmed.

After a while I tried to teach again. I had to tell them. It was like ... "What were you doing between those years?" "Well I was farming." "Why were you farming if you're such a damn good teacher?" As long as I dealt with kids, and kids included college people, they don't want me. They are scared I'm going to ... What am I going to do with them? They won't even take time to consider the fact that the only person I might ever hurt is myself. I am not going to hurt a child ... I worked with some women, and they said they admired the fact that I went on to college. I said, "Look, I have a mental illness, I am not mentally stupid!" There is nothing the matter with me.

Of course I did have something happen that they don't do any more. Without my permission but with my parents' permission ... thinking it was going to help, and I sort of dislike them for doing it ... they allowed me to undergo a series of 12 shock treatments. I do have times when I don't ... things just escape me, totally escape. There's a full year of my life I don't remember. But then I think, it wasn't that great a year, what am I worried about? But whenever I got some substitute teaching, whenever I walked back into history classes, I was worried. I mean so much depended upon your ability to think, and your ability to reason. And I didn't miss a beat! Now I might not know how to button my shirt, but by-darn I knew the darn history.

Before being diagnosed, I had just received an advancement. I was up for being a full professor, even without my PhD. I was working on my PhD. And then whenever that happened I just stopped. I never did go ahead and get my PhD. Why? Why get a PhD and sit on the tractor? My dad used to say, "If you went to school one more year, you'd be a blooming idiot." And he was serious. He never did understand that what I had I couldn't help. He seemed to believe that a lot of going to school is what caused this. And so he was not very ... well, whenever I'd say, I'd like to go back to school, he'd say, "Well, you won't be able to do it." And maybe he was right ... but I don't think so ... still taking the lousy pills, but I don't worry too much about it.

After being diagnosed, Louise returned to the farm. As she notes, a couple of times she thought about teaching again, or returning to university, but her desire was always curtailed by her father, other professionals or her own fears. She was weird for wanting too much education; and in her father's eyes her education caused her illness. One can not hear such a story without recalling the historical "rationale" for not allowing women into education – it would be too much for them; they are too irrational; it will cause them to be hysterical and mentally ill.[14] Likewise contemporary right-wing Christianity is concerned that too much education, particularly about feminism, could lead women to forget their "place." Women that ask for too much, that want a life away from home, deserve to be put in their place – by employers, husbands, and fathers. As a consequence, Louise's life is now one of isolation. She has been isolated by society and, in turn, has isolated herself. In her world, her internal world, she remains strong in the knowledge that she could do more; that she is capable of more; that she is intelligent; that she has a lot to offer. Nevertheless, her frustration at society's ignorance about mental illness is restrained by the fear that "they" might be right. For me, there is nothing more frightening than our ability to internalize oppression.

When my dad died, I farmed half a section, and when he died my cousin owned all the equipment. Well I had the option – do I want to buy all his equipment and continue? And I thought no I don't. I am at the age, I'm fifty someodd years old, I don't want to buy equipment and continue to farm. I farmed for my parents – that's as simple as that. Because I didn't want to. That wasn't my joy in life, to farm. I inherited it. That's one of the reasons I fixed up the house. I want to hold on to it, but then I'm it. It boils down to that. My cousin sitting up there, he's never married, and I've never married. We are both sitting on the family land that's going to go "phht" when we die.

Someone asked me, "Are you afraid to stay out there?", and I said, "Well, it's home." I said, "That's what makes the difference. But as long as I'm never scared I'll be all right." But there's so much stuff going on now, that you just ... I've got a rifle out there but it's for things I have to kill ... I was working some stuff down in the barn there, and I could just barely see this thing ... I had just a little old light. I thought it was a raccoon. So I came to the house and I got my flash light and I went back down, and it was a rattle-snake. And I thought, well, I'm not going to try and kill him with a hoe because I can't see that well. But then I thought, well I can't leave him, he'll get me. So I got my .22 and went out there and I shot ... I started shooting hoping he would run into the bullets, and I finally killed him. And he was about as big round as my arm, and he was about four feet long. He was just so big. After I saw him it scared me to death. And, like I said, I had that little old bitty light in there, it was just an old bulb and I tell you what, I light up the whole world down there now!

I've got a large family but I never see them. I'm different. For a long time I think they were jealous of the relationship that my dad and I had. I never see them. I don't see anybody as far as that goes. I see my cousin drive by, that's about it. I have a job delivering newspapers. I drive over 200 miles a day. Me and the dogs delivering papers. I would see some people whenever they would pay me, but that's it. Most people assume, family and people all around here, that I have wasted my education because I'm not teaching, not knowing *why* I'm not teaching.

So what. I haven't wasted anything, it's all here. I use it [her education] when I wish and I don't have to answer to anybody else. I didn't ask them to pay for it. I didn't ask them to work for it. And I don't owe them anything.

In the early evening, as I walked toward the car, Louise pointed out different parts of her farm. The air was cool and we could smell a good rainstorm brewing. She was planning her work for the next day – repairing some fence around her house. She looked toward the horizon, paused and spoke softly, "My dad used say, 'don't take a fence down until you know why it went up'." Her fences protect her. From other people's fear, and from her own. I can understand why she built hers. Society had already erected one around her.

Social fences are erected to keep out the unwanted, the unacceptable. Teri learned that she could only stray so far from social norms if she wanted to benefit from inclusion. Louise had little choice about her exclusion. When given a choice all of us would choose not to be discriminated against, demonized, marginalized. This desire is so great that sometimes it obliterates all other desires. Inclusion becomes paramount, particularly when it determines salvation. To be included in the Southern Christian community means adhering to God-given interpretations of gender. The final story in this section is about one woman's struggle to pattern her life on Christian gender norms, and the miracle that saved her from social exclusion.

In south Texas, I stopped to speak with a new evangelical pastor who, upon hearing about the content of the book, suggested that I speak with a local woman. She had grown up in the town, coached basketball in the area and a few years ago set up a working farm/ ranch for "delinquents" – city kids who had gotten into trouble with the law. J.T. was standing on her front porch as I drove up. She looked, well, quite frankly, she looked like a butch dyke in drag; I mean she was big, tough-looking, leather-skinned woman, but had "big hair," a clumsy make-up job, and painted nails on what were, upon closer inspection, quite callused hands. One look at her body and I knew exactly why the local preacher had suggested this interview. We settled down with a glass of iced tea and she began telling me about her life. Growing up in this small town, she had

frequently struggled with her difference. After college she became a
high-school basketball coach and taught mostly around the neighboring towns. Teachers, like preachers and their families, are
constantly subjected to public judgment about their private lives.
So J.T., who had not married, who did not look like the "lady"
teachers, found herself isolated and her sexuality often questioned.
Eventually she gave up coaching and returned home, establishing
the ranch as a place where she could combine her love of the
outdoors with her skills of working with young people. A couple of
years ago, she even got married:

> I just probably have a lifestyle of a person who chooses not to – a
> female who chooses not to – marry in pursuit of a career – a career
> predominantly male like coaching. It's not a big issue in the '90s,
> but in the '60s I was really a fish out of water. It was something I
> wanted to do – I wanted to coach because I had a coach when I was
> in school, a female coach, who was a major influence in my life.
> Before that time I had male coaches and they never took the time to
> really coach and teach ... show you that it's not about how good
> an athlete you are, it's about being the best you can be, whatever
> that is. I got a scholarship to go to play college women's basketball.
> We were just really different, you know. There was only 12 teams in
> the nation. Coming from that far back in the development of
> women's sport in America – all of us was considered homosexual
> whether we were or not. Just because we liked male things ... and
> because of my love of horses which is another male dominated area.
>
> Anyway when you're a coach you live a different lifestyle ...
> people expect you to be normal. The community you work for, or
> you live in, puts you on a pedestal, especially in the Bible Belt ... it
> is like if you were a nun. And if you don't play that role you can
> forget having your job, which is totally wrong. Not that I don't
> agree ... if you're coaching you shouldn't be out there sleeping with
> someone unless you're married to them. The point is that should not
> be why you lose your job. But in the Bible Belt that would definitely
> cost you your job.
>
> I have had the image of being abnormal and I have been called
> gay, lesbian all my life and I never have been. But I have been called
> that just because of ... I guess the lifestyle that I chose. I have

always felt like because of that I'd probably tend to fight for those people's rights – even though I don't believe in their lifestyle myself. I believe that they are going to have to handle it with their Savior the day it comes to their judgment. The day He opens their book, that's between Him and them. It's not for me to judge. While they don't force their lifestyle on me, fine, then I won't force mine onto them.

Probably the most controversial thing I have done recently, I married a man who was a known bisexual. He didn't go around flaunting it or anything, but, people who knew him knew that he had some sexual ideas, differences, compared to most men. But he is a very sensitive, very kind person, showered me with gifts and love. We never argued. In fact, I tell you, you know, since I got married it, my uneasiness in the small town, has got better.

When my marriage failed, I had never failed anything in my life. Eventually I came to the realization that it was not that *I* had failed. I had nothing to do with it. I might have been able to change or alter some parts of my marriage, but I was not in control of a person. Dad was very angry and the typical protective father and said, "Well, this is not good, but if you can't fix it, then you have to learn to live with it." I have a male friend, he's just a friend. He would love to be a boyfriend. We work on that relationship but I'm trying to keep that from happening because I'm not interested at all.

My dad never went to church, he was a mason. I never saw him in church except when my sister got married. Ma took us to Sunday school and church. I had a real strong female figure as a mother. My mother was a very strong woman, and did her own thing – a rancher. That's something else I do, you know, not a female thing, raise cattle, be a rancher.

So her hometown, and employers, had thought J.T. was a lesbian. She was in a male profession and was a rancher. Obviously, marrying had helped her be more accepted in the town, and presumably by her father. When her husband left her, and, she later noted, died of an AIDS-related illness, she became worried about how "the sexuality" question would continue to impact upon her life. She did not want to discuss her own sexuality; she simply noted that she had nothing against "those people" and that their "lifestyle" would be for God to judge. I then asked her how she approached problems facing young people who may question their sexuality:

> Oh yes, girls and boys are like night and day to work with. Girls are all emotional and cry and get upset easily and don't reveal their emotions for ten days, two weeks, and then they blow up. Boys talk to you, and it's over. That's basically the big difference. I love work- ing with the boys and the girls, not necessarily at the same time. But you can't work in a strictly male or female facility without dealing with the homosexuality ... kids acting out homosexually. We've not had big issues over that yet. I'm sure it will happen because every facility goes through that – of handling boys acting out sexually, or girls with girls – because sexuality is part of your body, part of your life and that's something that you have to deal with. We watch very carefully. We try to avoid letting any situation get set up that would create that – I try to keep the kids so tired that it doesn't happen.
>
> One of the good things about the rural Bible Belt is that it instills in young people the knowledge that they can do things ... some city kids never get that in their growing up period. They don't get that kind of self-esteem molded into their character. Even though I was a young woman in a man's world doing the teaching and the coach- ing, I had had such a strong background from my parents. They convinced me I could do things, you know, because they had been so solid, rock solid. There's some very positive things about growing up in a town where your family is rooted and are founding fathers of the town so to speak. I have been blessed by having good parents who were community leaders.

Obviously the social positioning of her parents had influenced her life. They were good, hard-working ranchers. Not necessarily well educated or middle class, but pillars of the community. I pushed her a bit more: had this affected how she understood her sexuality? Women could be ranchers and coaches, how did that sit alongside the gender roles taught by her pastor? She confided that after long talks with him, she realized that although she was not interested in finding another husband, she could be a good Christian woman by instilling "good" values in the young people with whom she worked. She attends church regularly and in the past few years, has seen the advantages of traditional women's roles. And in her mind, God had rewarded her – she became a mother, on Christmas Eve:

> I believe so strongly that there is no such thing as good luck and bad luck. I believe in being blessed. I honestly believe that. One Christmas Eve a former student turned up on my door step with a niece, 14 years old, who was pregnant. They didn't have the money to raise the child so she asked me if I would like to raise the child, adopt the child. After talking with them I thought about it over-night, and then agreed. I told them that I would provide a good home, medical care for this child during her pregnancy. That night I decided that if this child was born a boy his name would be Joseph and if the child was born a girl I would call her Mary.
>
> I don't have close contact with them [the mother], but I signed a deal that the birth mother could have contact. I've never heard from her. I was the first one to hold her; the first one to bathe her; the first one to feed her; the first one to diaper her; so she's like mine. Well, she is mine. To me that was just a blessing. There is no other way to explain it, except the Lord took me to do his work. The Lord gave me the opportunity to be an influence for my former student. She remembered me and she trusted me. I mean this child has been nothing but a blessing.

It is not unusual for a parent to think of a child as a blessing. But given J.T.'s social marginalization, and her desire to not be seen as a sexual misfit, having a baby appear on her door step – having "God grant her" the ultimate signifier of heterosexual womanhood – it is no wonder she feels blessed. As a singular narrative, it may be a story of God's blessing. Placed in the context of her life, it is also about her salvation. Perhaps salvation as defined by the local pastor. Perhaps for J.T., salvation from her "deviant" self. She has become a regular churchgoer, a carer of young people, and, miraculously, a concerned mother. She is no longer an isolated "other." She has been saved from "difference."

Each of these women, for they are not ladies, have done their best to do what society has asked of them in spite of their inability, or because of their desire, to do so. Southern ladies are privileged either because of their class – they have money to purchase the apparel of ladies – or because of their religious humility – they know that men are divinely sanctioned as the head of the household, and beyond. As noted above, historically the farmwife is a working-class woman unable to claim social superiority. Her difference, the need for her to be strong, likewise may cause her to question male superiority. So, how might they prove themselves worthy of social acceptance? It is not surprising that in the three stories above these women of difference speak about their relationship to children. Teri felt unable to continue bull riding after she married and had children. Louise resigned herself to complete social isolation because society, in the form of psychiatry, had told her to give up teaching – that she was a danger to children. And it was the blessing of motherhood that offered J.T. the social acceptance previously denied her. They remain proud, independent women who have rebelled as far as they dare. While they may never be ladies, they continue to struggle for survival in a hostile culture. They may never embrace feminism as a political movement questioning the normalization of patriarchy. But they do struggle with the uncomfortableness of patriarchy every day. And, in the words of Molly Ivins, "if that ain't class, you can kiss my grits."

THE BIBLE TELLS US SO

As we discovered in the previous chapter, each man has a different interpretation of masculinity. However, by listening to their stories, and knowing the religious, and racial, culture of the South, we can get a pretty good picture of what men think "manhood" is. Likewise, Southern ladies are struggling to make sense out of the historical legacy of Southern patriarchy and the dominance of Christian interpretations of gender. In doing so, they tell stories of who they are in relation to God, men, and the larger social structure. Even though one is not born a lady, they all know they should become one.

And if for some reason they find that difficult, or impossible, they are left feeling second best – internalizing the socio-religious rules which tell them they should remain isolated, marginalized, or do everything in their power to conform. God, we are told, wanted it that way. We should be "subject to our husbands" (Ephesians 5:21), submissive to their will. We should be "good wives" (Proverbs 31:10) cooking, cleaning, sewing, managing domestic life, teaching our children, caring for all the family, and beautiful. All of the women here know it. They know it and resign themselves to do it, or struggle to marry their wifely duties with their individual desires, or they struggle simply to survive.

Women are to be wives. They are also to be mothers. A woman who has children has credibility, social acceptance, as a woman – if she is a mother she is somehow categorized as an acceptable (tamed) woman.[15] A woman who does not have a relationship with a child is unacceptable – Louise was not labeled a *woman* with mental health problems, she was labeled a pariah. A child makes demands on a woman's time, and in doing so can control her – keep her relegated away from positions of power. That is why many women end up in part-time, low paid jobs; why they are passed over for promotion if they have children; why society tells women that a child will suffer if she enters the job market. Not having a child gives a woman a chance to be in control of her own time, possibly even to choose to enter, and compete in, the male marketplace. It is difficult for a woman to make those kinds of choices if she has an unplanned child. Once upon a time in the South, came a demand for a woman's right to make such choices.

NOTES

1 M. Ivins, *Molly Ivins Can't Say That, Can She?* (New York: Vintage Books, 1992), p. 166.

2 This section has relied largely upon C. A. Farnham (ed.), *Women of the American South* (New York: New York University Press, 1997). Also see J. Friedman, *The Enclosed Garden: Women and Community in the Evangelical South 1830–1900* (Chapel Hill, NC: University Press, 1985); and E. Fox-Genovese, *Within the Plantation Household: Black*

and White Women of the Old South (Chapel Hill, NC: University Press, 1988).

3 N. Silber, "The Northern Myth of the Rebel Girl," in Farnham (ed.), *Women of the American South*, pp. 122, 128.

4 The former speaker of the House of Representatives.

5 For more on the Christian Right's expectations of women, see D. Newman, *Then God Created Woman* and J. Dobson, *What Wives Wish Their Husbands Knew About Women*, both published by Focus on the Family and Tyndale, Colorado Springs, Colorado, 1998.

6 N. Silber, "The Northern Myth of the Rebel Girl," in Farnham (ed.), *Women of the American South*, pp. 122, 128.

7 J. S. De Hart, "Second Wave Feminism(s) and the South: The Difference that Differences Make," in Farnham (ed.), *Women of the American South*, p. 281.

8 *Ibid.*, p. 280.

9 "Stand by Your Man: The Ladies Memorial Association and the Reconstruction of Southern White Manhood," in Farnham (ed.), *Women of the American South*, p. 141.

10 *Ibid.*, p. 144.

11 H. Hagler, *The Journal of Southern History* 46 (1980), pp. 405–18.

12 T. Lockley, "A Struggle for Survival: Non-Elite White Women in Lowcountry Georgia, 1790–1830," in C. A. Farnham (ed.), *Women of the American South*, pp. 26–42. For a general discussion of similar issues, see S. Jeffreys, *The Spinster and her Enemies: Feminism and Sexuality 1880–1930* (London: Pandora, 1985).

13 M. Ivins, *Molly Ivins Can't Say That, Can She?*, pp. 69–70.

14 For further reading see P. Chesler, *Women and Madness* (New York: Avon Books, 1972); M. Foucault, *Madness and Civilization: A History of Insanity in the Age of Reason* (London: Tavistock, 1967) and *The Order of Things* (London: Tavistock, 1970); S. Gilbert and S. Gubar, *The Madwoman in the Attic: The Woman Writer and the Nineteenth Century* (New Haven, CN: Yale University Press, 1979); J. Ussher, *Women's Madness: Misogyny or Mental Illness* (London: Harvester Wheatsheaf, 1991); J. Ussher and P. Nicolson (eds), *Gender Issues in Clinical Psychology* (London: Routledge, 1991).

15 For an introduction to feminist perspectives on motherhood, see

A. Rich, *Of Woman Born: Motherhood as Experience and Institution* (London: Virago, 1977); N. Chodorow, *The Reproduction of Mothering: Psychoanalysis and the Sociology of Gender* (Berkeley, CA: University of California Press, 1978).

Chapter Four

CHOOSING LIFE

I call heaven and earth to record this day against you, that I have set
before you life and death, blessing and cursing: therefore choose life,
that both thou and thy seed may live ...   (Deuteronomy 30:19)

This right of privacy, whether it be founded in the Fourteenth
Amendment's concept of personal liberty and restrictions upon state
action, as we feel it is or, as the District Court determined, in the
Ninth Amendment's reservation of rights to the people, is broad
enough to encompass a woman's decision whether or not to terminate
her pregnancy.

(1973, Justice Blackmun, United States Supreme Court
majority opinion, *Roe* v. *Wade*, 410 US 113)

On January 22, 1973 the United States Supreme Court ruled, in a
seven to two decision, that the Texas anti-abortion statutes violated
the constitutional right to privacy. The judicial system had taken
almost three years to reach a final decision in *Roe* v. *Wade*. It was
too late for "Jane Roe." Her only choice was to give birth. And
then, unable to take care of the child, to choose to give it up for
adoption. But for thousands of other women the choice to
terminate an unwanted pregnancy became a guaranteed right.
Twenty years later *Roe* v. *Wade*, and what it stands for, remains a
central focus point for right-wing political activism. In American
politics, nothing divides the "Right" from the "Left" more than the
issue of abortion. While a woman's right to choose had substantial
political and religious support in the 1970s,[1] a now significant
proportion of the population believe abortion to be murder, even
genocide.

This chapter looks at the personal stories of key figures in the abortion debate. Sarah Weddington was an inexperienced young lawyer when she and colleague, Linda Coffee, filed the class action suit challenging the Texas anti-abortion laws. The day she stood in front of the United States Supreme Court, Sarah Weddington's career was made. The tenets of her argument set the framework for a national discussion over the extent of women's rights. But her involvement in the case was not about ambition. Unknown to anyone, it was about her own experience of a dirty, backroom abortion somewhere in a Mexican town. Her victory sparked a fierce backlash from the Christian Right. The most important, or the most vocal, mouthpiece of this anti-abortion crusade is Flip Benham and his "soldiers" in Operation Rescue. As its national director, Flip persuasively argues that abortion is murder. Murder that must be stopped. Operation Rescue conducts endless campaigns against abortion clinics, and their doctors. Many of these have led to criminal harassment charges, which have cost Flip Benham and Operation Rescue millions in fines. Other campaigns, committed by supporters of Operation Rescue but not condoned by it, have led to the murder of doctors who conduct abortions.

The central figure from the beginning, and now back in the limelight, is a working-class lesbian from Texas, Norma McCorvey, the "Jane Roe." As an unwed, unemployed young woman Norma became pregnant for a second time. After the birth of her first child, Norma's mother, believing her to be an unfit parent, took the baby to raise. During her second pregnancy Norma sought an abortion. A contact in Dallas put her in touch with Sarah Weddington and Linda Coffee. Years later, as an employee of an abortion clinic in Dallas, Norma met Flip Benham. Operation Rescue had set up its offices next door to the clinic and every time Benham saw Norma he reminded her of the central role she played in the "killings." After weeks listening to Benham's message, Norma came to believe. In August 1995 Norma was baptized as a new Christian and employed at Operation Rescue. I briefly met her during my interview with Benham. I was not permitted to interview her. But the sketch of her life, from her own writings and news interviews, along with Weddington's and Benham's commentary, illustrate the intensity of this debate, the logic of each side, and the difficulty facing every woman, particularly in the Bible Belt, of making such a "choice."

Before considering the lives, and beliefs, of these three figures I want to briefly rehearse the kinds of legal questions raised during *Roe* v. *Wade*, and around abortion more generally. An adequate literature review of the abortion debate would take an entire book. Such is not my task here. Instead I want simply to highlight the arguments used to rationalize either side of this "pro-life" *v.* "pro-choice," or as some would have it, "anti-abortion" *v.* "pro-abortion," debate. Two important questions underpin these positions: when does life begin – at conception or at birth? And does a woman have the right to terminate a pregnancy?

During the Supreme Court hearings, the State of Texas [*Wade*] argued that life begins at the moment of conception and therefore it had a duty to protect prenatal life. In his important work on *The Right to Privacy*, Vincent Samar summarizes the State's position in *Roe* v. *Wade*. "The State of Texas argued that the statutes were justified by the state's legitimate interest to (1) discourage illicit sexual conduct, (2) protect the life and health of the mother, and (3) protect prenatal life."[2] Representing "Roe," Sarah Weddington argued that the State did not treat the fetus as a person/citizen with legal rights, nor did abortions require a death certificate. Therefore the State did not have precedent legislation which considered conception as the beginning of life, or citizenship. Weddington recalls her argument in her book *A Question of Choice*: "The Constitution ... attaches protection to the person at the time of birth. Those persons born are citizens."[3] The Court agreed with Weddington that the State should not consider that life or citizenship began at conception.

However, the judges were unwilling to declare that life only began at birth. "When those trained in the respective disciplines of medicine, philosophy, and theology are unable to arrive at any consensus, the judiciary, at this point in the development of man's knowledge, is not in a position to speculate as to the answer."[4] Abortion might be acceptable at eight weeks, but not at eight months. In the majority opinion, Justice Blackmun relied upon a medical analysis of pregnancy, dividing it into trimesters. During the first three months, "the abortion decision and its effectuation must be left to the medical judgment of the pregnant woman's attending physician." During the second, "the State, in promoting its interest in the health of the mother, may if it chooses, regulate the abortion procedure in ways that are reasonably related to maternal health." In the final three months of pregnancy, "the State, in promoting its interest in the potentiality of human life, may, if it chooses, regulate, and even proscribe, abortion except where it is necessary, in appropriate medical judgment, for the preservation of the life or health of the woman." The State, it turned out, does have an interest in the unborn – "in protecting the potentiality of human life."

Concerning the second question, Weddington argued that the Fourteenth and Ninth Amendments did guarantee a right to privacy which could include a woman's right to choose the termination of her pregnancy. The Court agreed, but, like the right to free speech, this was not an absolute right:

> This right of privacy, whether it be founded in the Fourteenth Amendment's concept of personal liberty and restrictions upon state action, as we feel it is, or, as the District Court determined, in the Ninth Amendment's reservation of rights to the people, is broad enough to encompass a woman's decision whether or not to terminate her pregnancy. The detriment that the State would impose upon the pregnant woman by denying this choice altogether is apparent ...
>
> ... Appellants and some *amici* argue that the woman's right is absolute and that she is entitled to terminate her pregnancy at whatever time, in whatever way, and for whatever reason she alone chooses. With this we do not agree. Appellants' arguments that Texas either has no valid interest at all in regulating the abortion decision, or no interest strong enough to support any limitation upon the woman's sole determination, is unpersuasive. The Court's

decisions recognizing a right of privacy also acknowledge that some state regulation in areas protected by that right is appropriate. As noted above, a state may properly assert important interests in safeguarding health, in maintaining medical standards, and in protecting potential life. At some point in pregnancy, these respective interests become sufficiently compelling to sustain regulation of the factors that govern the abortion decision. The privacy right involved, therefore cannot be said to be absolute ... We therefore conclude that the right of personal privacy includes the abortion decision, but that this right is not unqualified and must be considered against important state interests in regulation.[5]

So a woman's right to privacy can include her right to choose to terminate an unwanted pregnancy. And as long as this choice is exercised within the first trimester, legal abortions should be available in a clean, healthy environment. For the present time, this ruling seems to have settled the legality of these two questions: life begins after the first trimester and women, during that trimester, do have the right to choose to end a pregnancy. But legal clarity is not always accompanied by moral certainty.

Rights, even those that are guaranteed, when acted upon are not always considered acceptable moral behavior by the majority. The South in particular is known for not upholding the rights of some, even if Yankee courts tell them to. And Christianity is known for moral crusades against sin becoming an accepted social norm. The resulting communal pool of values turns into raging waters indeed. So I went to talk with Sarah Weddington and Flip Benham about their involvement in this socio-moral storm. Unsurprisingly perhaps, they both live in Texas. Moreover, they both seem to believe in the guiding hand of a higher power. There may be only one God, but He has certainly led Sarah and Flip in opposite directions.

VISITING WITH SARAH

Assuming I would get lost in the big city, I arrived a little early in downtown Austin for my appointment with Sarah. But unlike most capital cities, the center of Austin resembles a small county seat.

There are few skyscrapers; the tree-lined residential streets simply give way to the patch of grass where the capital building is located. Now of course everything is bigger in Texas. And I am told that the dome of the building is the highest of any capital, including the White House. But the climate is not, as one might expect of Texas' capital, that of macho power. Maybe that is because the land for the capital was originally donated by the University of Texas located just a few blocks north. Its proximity to a well-respected, and mildly liberal, university gives the capital an air of toleration, of calm rational government that, if you know anything about Texas history, just ain't reality. The whole place is a façade. How could this be the capital of Texas? For heaven's sake, there is a substantial gay village, and generally "alternative" community just a few blocks away! If I had rolled down the window I am sure the air would have been patchouli oil not crude and cowshit. I even saw a couple of women with nose rings. This may be Texas, but not as I know it.

Sarah's office was equally disturbing. Any respectable legal star would surely have a penthouse, oak-filled office. I had to be lost. I drove around the block again, checked the street signs, asked a girl on the corner, got out, walked by the address. When the appointed time came, I tentatively rang the door bell of the cutest little wooden house fully expecting grandma to answer. But sure enough, Sarah herself opened the door. The office consisted basically of three large rooms on the ground floor of a renovated cottage – one for the secretary, one for the files and one, the front room, for Sarah. We settled into a couple of high back living room chairs, checked the tape recorder and began. My expectation that Austin would be the cowboy Mecca was only surpassed by my expectations about meeting Sarah Weddington. Around the age of 15 I published a newsletter for preachers' kids, a kind of support network for kids whose lives in the parsonage often isolated them from "normal" kids. Even with the help of donations, circulation only reached about 1500. One of those donations came from a retired preacher's wife who enclosed a letter about how she wished her kids, who were now grown, would have benefited from such support. It was only a few lines. At the bottom she simply said, "perhaps you have heard of my daughter Sarah Weddington. She was the lawyer for *Roe* v. *Wade*." Of course I didn't have a clue what she was talking about. It was only after I enrolled at McMurry University did I hear again of the legendary Sarah Weddington. So, we were both preachers' daughters and both now alumni of the same little liberal arts college in the middle of nowhere. While the reason for the interview was her role in *Roe* v. *Wade*, there was another agenda. I wanted to know about her, about her relationship with her parents, her religious beliefs, her career, her life. A lot to expect in a one-hour interview.

So before I met with her I picked up her book *A Question of Choice*, written just a few years ago.[6] In it she reviews her legal arguments as well as the history of the case's journey to the Supreme Court. She also writes about her life. So I had a general picture to go on. One thing was clear. Her life had, to a large extent, been defined by her involvement with this case. Some would like to believe that Sarah took on the case because she saw it as a way to make her career; that she couldn't care less about Norma McCorvey; that she hardly even spoke to Norma during the appeals process. We will get to the intricacies of their relationship later. The bottom line was that Norma did not want to be pregnant and abortions were illegal in Texas. As a working-class, uneducated woman Norma knew she could not care for the child, and that she did not want to go through another adoption. Weddington knew this was Norma's situation, and the situation of thousands like her. She filed a "class action" suit so that a favorable ruling would help every woman. So Sarah was not only representing Norma, she was representing an idea about women's rights and, as she admits later, Sarah was representing herself.

As a young law student with a steady boyfriend, Sarah became pregnant. She remembers being "a scared graduate student in 1967 in a dirty, dusty Mexican border town to have an abortion, fleeing the law that made abortion illegal in Texas."[7] *Roe* v. *Wade* was not, as some would like to believe, about an eager young lawyer trying to make her mark. What is clear throughout her book is that this case reflected her own pain, her own experience of the abhorrent medical conditions in which illegal abortions took place. Of course this was not part of *Roe* v. *Wade*. In fact until the publication of *A Question of Choice* in 1992, only Sarah and her boyfriend-now-husband knew about her abortion. Her deep conviction that a woman has the right to make choices about her own life grew out of her own life experiences:

In the book you speak openly about your personal life. Certainly becoming a lawyer challenges roles for women, did you get the support that was needed from family and teachers?

I think the hardest part was that I knew no women attorneys. I was in Munday and Canyon, Texas, during those formative years and to my knowledge there were no women attorneys there. I don't remember reading about a woman attorney. So the only attorney I actually knew was a member of our church who was a very close friend of the family and someone I really admired. But looking back I knew nothing about what he did. I just knew he was an attorney. And that's about the size of what I knew about that. I had been someone who questioned limits, even at McMurry [University]. For example, there was no dancing allowed at McMurry and so I led a crusade as an officer of the Student Association, because I thought there wasn't enough for McMurry students to do. They agreed we could have a "social function," but we could not call it a dance. We also questioned the limits on women's basketball and a variety of other things.

My parents actually were encouraging, my mother particularly. She was, in many ways, typical of a lot of preachers' wives who would really have been happier having a career as well as a family. She had taught women's basketball in Gorman, Texas, in a prior life. She later got her Masters in education and started in business school. She was really, to look back, much better suited to be a teacher or out in the work world. Instead she was told that her role as a preacher's wife would not allow that. So I think mother probably felt the restrictions of the role of a preacher's wife and that was probably one of the reasons she encouraged me to be involved in lots of different activities and was never discouraging about going to law school, and on the whole, I think encouraging. Daddy wasn't directly encouraging or discouraging, but more just saying, you know, whatever you want to do we'll support you in that and that kind of stuff. I really got serious about going to law school when I graduated in December from McMurry, and came down to Austin that spring semester to work at the legislature. I don't think it was something that I went and talked to a whole lot of people about. So much more than deciding, I didn't think I really wanted to teach eighth grade, didn't have enough chemistry for medical school, law school was something you could get into if you had very good grades. I did have good grades. I had been active in debate, extemporaneous speaking, a lot of other things. So, I think it was much more that it was something that I could get into, that seemed to be a good choice for me.

In the book you mention getting involved in a consciousness-raising group during law school. Was that one of the first times that you had come across women discussing issues that affected them?

Yes, I certainly have not ever experienced a consciousness-raising group before Austin. There were social groups, not sororities but social groups, on the McMurry campus and I have been a part of a group of women students. We had a lot of fun creating it, but it was certainly not consciousness-raising. I mean, there were issues about what it meant to be a woman and what our futures were but not in the same way. So Austin was my first experience of really consciousness-raising groups.

You also note that you were not an extremely active member of this consciousness-raising group. What kind of role did you take?

I think in terms of actually attending the consciousness-raising groups my role was more a listener than a leader. Others really had thought about the issues much more than I and so I listened. But because I was in law school, and then out of law school, I had the ability to go do research that nobody else could – except another woman who was a lawyer a little bit later. They just did not have the capacity to do that particular kind of research. So I would go and look up laws that had to do with marriage and age of marriage or what happened in the event of divorce – the various issues that were raised in terms of women being fairly treated.

When you started working on *Roe* v. *Wade* what was the reaction from your parents? Did you warn them that you were going to be working on this case?

No, I never asked their permission. There's an old, old saying – "Tis better to ask forgiveness than to ask permission" and so I just didn't. I didn't put the burden on them of being able to say "yes" or "no." I just went ahead and made my own plan. And then gradually I kept them informed. My mother did go to the Supreme Court hearing with me and daddy couldn't – I think he would have but he stayed home to take care of the other kids. There were never any really long serious discussions about whether I should be involved or anything like that. I think that might be partially because, for daddy, the position I was taking was fairly consistent with Methodist theology. I wasn't taking it for that reason, but certainly the Methodist position was that abortion should not be entered into lightly, that it should be legal and the Board of Christian Social Concern of the United Methodist Church filed a brief in our favor. I think by the time I was actually working on the case, dad was the District Superintendent, which meant he would get much less comment than if he had been in a rural church. But I never heard daddy say any comment at all, so whether there was or wasn't he never conveyed that to me.

In her book Sarah recalls telling her mother and father on the day the judgment was announced. Not unlike our conversation, Sarah seems to focus on her father's reaction. She simply notes that her mother was "pleased" then spends the rest of the paragraph outlining her father's "analytical" reaction. "I called mother and daddy, who were pastoring in Lubbock. The announcement probably meant more to mother, since she had been in the Supreme Court with me. She was pleased by what I had accomplished. Daddy's reaction was more analytical: he was glad I had won, of course, since I'd been working so long and diligently on the case; he was glad that we had won by a strong majority, so the issue was really decided and was no longer a question; he was pleased that the principles that he personally held and which I had represented had been approved by the Supreme Court; and he was glad that women would be no longer in back alleys but rather in safe surroundings under the watchful eyes of trained professionals."[8] From my own background experience, I can understand this need to ensure approval and agreement on ideological points from a father who is a preacher. And I know how important that becomes when you are uncertain about sharing a "secret" which may cause disapproval on those grounds. Remember, Sarah's parents never knew of her abortion until over 20 years after the case.

When you had an abortion did you tell friends or family members?

I never told anybody about it, nobody. My husband knew, that was all. And until I wrote the book absolutely no one knew.

What was the reaction of your parents once it came out in the book?

It was 25 years later. The reaction was very subdued, mother and daddy basically, they never mentioned it. They loved the book when they read it, I didn't really tell them. They read a preliminary draft, but really no discussion at all.

After the case, what kind of reaction did you get from friends, supporters and non-supporters?

When we won the case obviously I heard from detractors but those tended to be ugly letters and things like that. I certainly heard from supporters and they tended to be letters, phone calls, everybody was so excited about winning *Roe* v. *Wade*. So it was joyous, it was upbeat, it was wonderful. But if anybody had said to me then I'd still be talking about it in 23 years, I would say certainly never have believed it!

Do you still get mail from non-supporters?

It still comes, usually after I've done a debate or a speech of some kind, then I can anticipate getting some ugly mail.

When *Roe* v. *Wade* went before the Supreme Court weren't there a number of religious denominations supporting it?

Yes, I knew a few of those because of my Methodist connections. But there were actually a wide variety of ministers from Baptist, Jewish, Presbyterians. There was an *amicus curiae* brief filed in our favor by a wide variety of religious groups. Here in Texas at that point the Southern Baptists often were helping us. I didn't think of the Southern Baptists as enemies. I didn't think of the Catholics as being, you know, officially very opposed to abortion. There were a lot of groups I thought of as being friendly.

At the time were there religious groups that were organized around stopping you?

There were certainly some groups organized. They were not nearly so obviously religious-based as they are today. They were not nearly as organized as they are today. I think one political science lesson is simply that it's much easier to get people excited about changing something than it is to get them excited about keeping it just the way it is. So at that point we were the reformers, we were the ones trying to change it and I think probably the opposition had a harder time getting organized against us. Whereas today we have the harder time getting organized in favor of pro-choice and they have come to use certain religious groups, fundamental churches, Catholic churches, some Southern Baptist, much more. I mean they leaflet in the parking lots; they will have people from the lectern talk about the abortion issue. They have a way of finding their people every week, whereas we have no place our people are all together. Even though there are still a variety of religious groups that basically are in favor of abortion being legal, they are not using the churches to organize and proselytize in the ways those who are anti do now. Organized opposition is much greater now although there was some in the early days.

What do remember most about growing up as the daughter of a minister? How do the values you learned there relate to your work as a lawyer?

Actually I think it was very helpful. There's an old saying, Barbara Jordan [a] former member of Congress, said "To be a leader you must be comfortable feeling different." I think I said in the book that I am very sincere about it, I mean, if you are a preacher's kid, you always feel different. I think actually feeling different has been easier for me. Daddy was not a "hell and brimstone" person but he was much more the Gospel of Christian social concern, which said you have an obligation to care about a larger good and those kind of things. So I think that was a lot of what I learned. Also it was very true in growing up in the preacher's family that people were very supportive and so I would start being in the choir, playing the piano, doing the devotionals from a very early age. People were very encouraging about it, very positive about it, so I would do it again. I think a lot of the skills I learned in terms of oral presentations really go back to those days in a preacher's family. So I cannot imagine what it would have been like if my father had been a far different kind of preacher. But given who he was, it has certainly been a very positive thing for me.

After the interview Sarah offered me access to her files on gay and lesbian issues in Texas. As I moved into the file room a clerk came in with the relevant material, and I glanced up to see another dyke. Well she didn't actually say she was, but I have developed a pretty good sense about these things. And the arrival of an equally dykey "friend" a half hour later was proof enough for me. I finished with the files, and decided to have a quick look around. The hallway wall was covered with photographs. Given the decor I fully expected these to be family photos. But upon closer inspection they were all pictures of Sarah – and the Queen of England, and President Clinton, and Hillary, and ex-Governor Ann Richards, and ... and ... every major US political figure for the last 20 years. Being suitably impressed, all I could think was "one degree of separation" – me and Hillary!

Just outside of Austin city limits I slowly returned to the real Texas of rolling plains, cowboys in their pickup trucks, and, I rolled down the window to check, yes those lovely smells of nature. As I listened to the tape again, I noticed the fascination I seemed to have with Sarah's relationship with her father. On reflection this wasn't surprising, but I had been unaware of it during the interview. What had I expected her to say? What had I needed to hear? We had both acknowledged the strength of character we had received from our mothers. But there is something about having a father who everyone in the town looks to for advice, for direction, for hope when life gets too much. Lucky for us, our fathers had not been "hell and brimstone" preachers. Lucky for us, they believed Biblical lessons had to be interpreted, and learned, by each person, individually.

Christian values do, without a doubt, vary according to one's interpretation of Biblical texts. On the more liberal end of the scale, some Christian denominations leave a large amount of the interpretative process up to the individual. Determining Christian values becomes an individualized analysis of scripture, perhaps with a bit of guidance from theologians or denominational regulations and tempered by much prayerful consideration. As Weddington points out, Methodists often focus on a doctrine of social concern, or social justice. But this picture of Christianity is not one often associated with the Bible Belt. Instead what the most dominant force in the American South is, and increasingly so across the nation, is a right-wing version of Christianity with an extremely conservative interpretation of the Bible. According to this version of Christian values, life begins at conception. "Before I formed you in the womb I knew you, and before you were born I consecrated you." (Jeremiah 1:5.) It is not difficult to see that if one believes that life begins at conception then the termination of pregnancy is murder. It is the taking of human life. While recognizing that carrying pregnancy to term may cause financial and emotional difficulties for women who do not want a child, these difficulties cannot be compared to the tragedy of taking a human life. Justice, according to these Christian values, is stopping the murder of the unborn who cannot defend themselves. For some, this justice must be enforced by any means necessary. Officially, Operation Rescue does not condone killing of any kind. Supporters have, however, been arrested for harassment of doctors and other workers at abortion clinics. Somehow I had a feeling Flip Benham's office was not going to be a renovated cottage.

ON THE FLIPSIDE

The mission of Operation Rescue is explained in the pamphlet "The Way of the Cross: No Cheap Solutions":

> Operation Rescue unashamedly takes up the cause of preborn children in the name of Jesus Christ. We employ only Biblical principles. The Bible is our foundation. The Cross of Christ is our strategy; the repentance of the Church of Jesus Christ is our ultimate goal. As the Church changes its heart toward unborn children, God Himself will hear from heaven, forgive our sin, and bring healing to our land. We believe that Jesus Christ is the only answer to the abortion holocaust. It is upon our active repentance at abortion mills, abortionists' homes, churches, and practices that the Gospel is visibly lived out. We become to the church, to our city, and to our nation living parables which rightly represent God's heart toward His helpless children ... While the responsibility of others may be to seek to make abortion illegal, our Biblical mandate is to confront the church and our nation with the sin, the immorality, and the horror of abortion. This is our cross. We will carry it to the streets. We will carry it to the churches. We will carry it to the clinics. We will carry it to the hospitals that give sanctuary to child killers. We will continue to follow the way of the cross and the example of our Lord Jesus Christ as we rescue those being led away to slaughter. We must hold so tightly to the cross of Christ that there is no room to hold any other weapon.[9]

102

Flip Benham, national director of Operation Rescue, agreed to speak to me about the theology behind the project, about the extent of their support and political influence across the United States, and about how he came to play a role in the salvation of Norma McCorvey, "Jane Roe."

Driving up to the offices of Operation Rescue I felt a bit lost. I found the address easily enough. As a young dyke in Abilene I learned very quickly how to find my way around Dallas. It may have been 250 miles away, but it had the only decent gay village in the area. The street signs were definitely more familiar than those in Austin. Nevertheless I knew I was lost. The interview questions were well rehearsed, but I was much more nervous than I had been preparing to meet Sarah. She was like a celebrity to me. Flip, well meeting Flip was like entering the lion's den. I knew instinctively what he would be like – smooth, very smooth; and as eloquent as an angel. Not like a tele-evangelist – he wasn't for a second insincere. He believed. And I did too, at one time. Now, to him, I was lost.

The offices of Operation Rescue would not be plush; charities usually do not afford themselves public luxuries. But I did not expect the extensive bleakness which I found. Somewhere in north-east Dallas, I pulled onto an empty parking lot. The only buildings in sight looked like storage garages. On closer inspection a few of the doors displayed business names. One was a clinic. Next door a small sticker in the window simply noted the letters "OR." I parked the car and looked in the mirror. Why hadn't I worn make-up? He would know the minute he laid eyes on me: trousers, no bag, no lipstick, no hairspray. And this was Dallas for God's sake! He would definitely know. Play up the academic bit, the British bit, the preacher's daughter bit. And pray. I walked to the office door, prayed to St Daniel, and stepped into Flip's den.

He escorted me to a counseling room where I flicked through some brochures while waiting for him to return. There is a reason you never see pictures of aborted fetuses. Flip joined me and after explaining the project, I asked the first question. For the next 90 minutes I sat captured by his voice, by his logic, by his exuberant belief. Once in a while I caught a glimpse of the children's toys scattered about the room. Having the staff's children around the office was not just about employee relations; they were an effective weapon. Every time he said "murder," I saw the pictures again in my head, the toys at my feet. I tried to keep to the script. Afterwards he showed me around the office. Introduced me to Norma. Any journalist would have simply blurted out a few questions for her. I wanted to be back in my car, back in my ivory tower, back to a place where I could forget. Even now editing the tapes of him, hearing his voice again, a part of me can't help thinking he makes sense. A small part of me.

Can you tell me why you are pro-life?

Back in Genesis there was Adam and there was Eve. Then there entered another personality who was the serpent. The serpent tempted Adam and Eve and he did that by saying, "you can partake [of the tree of the knowledge]." God was simply depending upon the self-government of Adam and Eve not to do it, but the tempter caused them to do it. Their partaking of the tree of knowledge – of good and evil – means more than just knowing about it, it means that you *participate* in it, you become as God. *You* determine what is good and what is evil. From Genesis Chapter 3:15 onwards God tells us that there is going to be a battle going on between two seeds – the seed of the serpent and the seed of the woman. The seed of the serpent says "I am the master of my ship, the captain of my fate, I determine what is good, I determine what is evil." If you wanted to know a philosophical [equivalent] you would say "cogito ergo sum" – "I think therefore I am," René Descartes. [This] paints very beautifully the portrait that if a tree falls in the middle of a forest and nobody is around to hear it, then of course it doesn't make a sound because no one was there to perceive it. That is the seed of the serpent. That world view has been struggling against another world view called the seed of the woman. On that side it says that God is the center of the universe. It says "I am, therefore I think," John Locke. You'll find that in that scenario, in that world view, if a tree falls in the center of the forest and nobody is there to hear it, it makes a sound. Why? Because there are certain universal principles that apply that are morally absolute, they work whether I am there or not. In other words, the law of gravity is going to work whether I am around or not ... if I [choose] to disagree with it, there are certain consequences for the disagreement – of physical laws and of moral laws. So those two world views are battling. It [Genesis 3:15] says that he will bruise your heel; that's the seed of the serpent will bruise the heel. Of course the most beautiful way that that's lived out is that Jesus was nailed to a cross. He was wounded and bruised for our iniquities and transgression. But he crushed the head of the serpent, because you will wound his heel, but he will *crush* your head. That battle – those two world views – have been fighting each other and many colors of ideologies in between those. But it's always those two – one where man is the center, one where God is the center.

I think that in this nation we most clearly see the battle of those two world views over the issue of slavery in the mid-nineteenth century when, in 1857, in a seven-to-two decision, the Supreme Court declared that Blacks were non-persons. We just declared it, I mean it wasn't true, we just said it. It was the law of the land. There was the battle between the two world views. We did what we felt was right in our own eyes and of course there was a bloody civil war ... but finally the battle was won and as we look back now we would wonder how could anybody have said that Blacks were not people. But that's what many Christians and many people thought. It was the battle between two seeds.

In these days, in our nation we are finding that this battle is manifesting itself most clearly over the abortion issue. Once or twice in every century an issue arises that is so deep in its foundations that it requires every person to take a stand. This is one of those. That's why it's almost a litmus test. [If] I know where you stand on abortion, I know where you stand on everything else because I know what world you come from. See what I am saying? – that if I know that ... then I know everything that I need to know about you if I am going to vote for you to place you in office. In these days the seed of the serpent says, "my rights, my body, my choice, not the church, not the state, women must decide their fate." It is mine, me, I do it all myself – that's the seed of the serpent. Versus the seed of the woman which says, "you were bought with a price, you are not your own, therefore glorify God with your body." This body doesn't belong to me, Jesus paid a price for me and my gifts and everything that I'm given are to [be] given away to others. This battle is what is going on in this nation. It will not be solved politically. Abortion is pre-eminently a Gospel issue, a fight between two seeds. And as the heart of this nation again changes towards the children, the laws will reflect that change. That's always the way it is in politics – you have to deal with the heart and then the laws come. It's just a flat out fact – hate is a sin, it's not a crime. But hate can work out and manifest itself in crime, you know, in murder, in assault, or what have you. So if you want to deal with murder on the streets what do you do? Do you just try to rehabilitate it, or do you go into the heart of the matter and deal with the hate that causes the murder? Of course that is sin and that is something that a lot of folks don't want to deal with and that is why in our nation today we have violence just savaging the streets. You know [we hear about a recent case in America where a mother drowned her two children] and we're just aghast. How can a mother do that? But I just want you to know that it happens 4,400 times in our nation every single day as mothers do that. [That woman] did hers a little later than most of the mums.

What is the history of Operation Rescue?

Back in 1988 the first major rescues that you saw on national television were at the Democratic National Convention in Atlanta, Georgia. That's the first time that I saw a lady – an eighty-year-old lady – get arrested. I couldn't believe it. And she was the Baptist Sunday school teacher. I saw them dragging her off and throwing her in the paddy wagon. When I found out why they did it and what she had done [to be arrested] it just stunned me. I said that lady is living out *my* theology. It says in the Bible "Greater love has no man than this that he lay down his life for his friends" and she did that! So many, many, many of us got involved and now over 75,000 arrests have taken place in Operation Rescue-sponsored events all over the country. And through these years, there has not been one convicted act of violence, not one. Which makes Operation Rescue simply the most peaceful social revolution that has ever come to this county. It's peaceful precisely because it is governed by the Gospel of Christ, that we lay our lives down and not the life of another. Now there have been shootings in abortion mills, shootings – [killing doctors who perform abortions] – and that's a sad state of affairs. But when you move the peaceful protesters off the street you open up the door for vigilantism like that.

One of the best things you can do is have hundreds of Christians out on the streets. Whenever we go out, we go out with moms and dads, grandmas and grandpas, little boys and little girls – we go out with families. We're family folks. We love the family. God invented the family and so whenever we go out on the streets, we always go out with families. That brings safety not only for the little baby boys and girls who are going to be killed in those mills, because a lot of mums changed their minds, but also for those that are actually doing the killing. So Operation Rescue has been simply the wheels that bring the Church of Jesus Christ out of the church and brings it to the gates of our children that have been killed. That's what we are, we're simply a vehicle to get the church where it needs to be.

How extensive is the support for Operation Rescue?

We have a lot of faithful Christians because really you've got to be involved in this for more than the cause. It's got to be a Gospel issue. If you're in it for the cause – to save little children, you'll go crazy. You can't do it.

How many supporters do you have?

I don't want to tell you that, but I can tell you that there have been over 75,000 arrests, and most of the people out at the mills don't get arrested, so that might give you an idea of some of the numbers . . . This is the national center, and this is the center in Dallas. We have tons of them all over the place, but I would never . . . Oh, there are several of them, but I probably don't want to tell you, we get sued all the time. We just got sued the week before last for $8.6 million. I mean that's what Planned Parenthood does. It does everything it can to get us off the street and into the courtroom. They can win in the courtroom because the truth is censored but when we are on the street, we win the battle.

Why are they trying to get you off the streets?

Because we picketed a doctor and told the truth about him. [We] said that [he] not only delivers babies, he kills them. Because we did that on a public sidewalk, and did that for ten months – where he worked, where he killed children, at his Church and at his home – [always] on the public sidewalk – we were sued for $8.6 million . . . That's what's happening in America, all over the country, it's not just here. We were sued down in Houston, Texas for $1.1 million for praying on a public sidewalk across the street from the abortion mill. Free speech is free in this nation for anybody – for pornographers, for animal rights activists, for environmentalists. You can say whatever you want to say unless you are a Christian and you are going to say something about the humanity of those baby boys and girls, then its censored. You will notice that in every newspaper you will never see a picture of a baby that's been killed by abortion – *ever*. You will never see it on television because the truth is so devastating that if it gets out they'll probably stop doing it.

This is a deserted looking area, where are your supporters today?

We're out there, we're out there. They kill on Thursdays, Fridays and Saturdays, so you didn't see anything going on [day of interview was not one of those three days]. They ripped our sign off the wall. They don't want us to have a sign out there. But we have folks that are out there. It's called sidewalk counseling and we give moms a choice, we give them brochures. Then we offer them a place [to stay], like if the big bully boyfriend they're living with says "If you don't get an abortion you're not going stay with me." Some of these girls really feel like they have no choice at all. So we are there to open a window and say, "Hey, look instead of running away from Jesus you can run right into him and he can take what you think is a curse and turn it into such a wonderful blessing if you let him."

Do you believe that you have support across the nation?

Oh I think the majority of the nation is pro-life. I don't think there's any question about that. You see, we never would have had [legal abortions], and if somebody had to try [to] bring it to a vote in the Congress – as to whether or not we would do away with all the laws that protect children like the Supreme Court did in 1973 – it never would have happened. It never would have happened. Nobody ever would have done it. Unfortunately the Supreme Court has taken a very pro-active role in this. So just seven men made that decision, and it applied to everybody. I mean it was the most incredibly stifling thing that has ever happened. And if [they had] thought it [through] really hard then, it probably wouldn't be in place now. But we just let it go. Just like the Nazis did in Germany with the extermination of the Jews. It was just little by little by little and the government kept going a little further and further and then finally there was [Auschwitz].

One of the brochures I glanced through in the office addressed the impact of abortions on the Black population in America. A number of the points made in the brochure, entitled "Abortion: The Black Woman's Voice" and published by Texas Black Americans for Life, explicitly refer to the "racism" of the pro-choice movement.[10] For example, the opening comment notes greater percentages of abortions amongst minority women: "[They] constitute only about 26% of the female population (age 15–44) in the United States, but they underwent approximately 36% of the abortions." One woman included in the brochure, Dr Dolores Grier, psychologist and president of American Black Women Against Abortion, argues that abortions are being used by the white population to stay in the majority: "Since 1973, 78% of abortion centers have been located in Black and minority communities. Upper middle class white females are not reproducing and they are trying to keep other groups from reproducing so they can remain in the majority." Another woman, Akua Furlow, executive director of Life Education and Resource Network, attack Planned Parenthood specifically: "Planned Parenthood started back in 1960 by Margaret Sanger. If people would just study the documentation they would find that Planned Parenthood was rooted in racism and founded by a white supremacist. She believed there were dysgenic groups of

people who needed to be exterminated. Most of Planned Parenthood's clinics are in minority communities. The language has
changed, but the original intent is still the same – to limit the births
of minority people, poor people, people that are handicapped." So I
asked Benham about the relationship between abortion and racism:

What do you think of the argument that legal abortions support racism?

Well, yes ... of course Margaret Sanger [founder of Planned Parenthood] herself
was a racist and a eugenicist, she was for the Third Reich. Of course all of the
liberal elite was for the Third Reich in [relation to] eugenics, at least in the study of
the master race kind of a thing. As a matter of fact, she called her project Planned
Parenthood the "Negro Project" and she termed them – "blacks, human weeds
that need to be destroyed." She said "we must have more people from the fit and
less from the unfit." These are quotes of Margaret Sanger, who's a founder of
Planned Parenthood. So if the root is bad, the founder is bad, you can expect that
everything else is. She's a huge embarrassment for Planned Parenthood now, just
her quotes rip them apart. So they try and cover up everything they can. They still
present the Maggi Award, that's the Margaret Sanger Award, but it's a sad, sad
thing. Of course Margaret Sanger was a racist.

And it's interesting to me that in the "Negro Projects" she used the Black
pastors to begin to talk to the folks about the benefits of birth control. You see it
was all a "birth control" kind of a thing. Why control the birth of Blacks? You know,
because "less from the unfit more from the fit." They were human weeds ... it's a
racist thing ... So we can see it's genocide – it's a genocidal thing that the Blacks
don't know.

Another one of the pamphlets produced by Operation Rescue sets
out a strong political agenda. After reading "Jesus is the Standard,"
there is no doubt what Operation Rescue believes is the single most
important political issue:

> Today, some politicians are compromising their pro-life position in
> the hope it will gain them a political advantage. What's even more
> incredible, is that many actually believe they can betray the Chris-
> tian community, the pro-life movement, the unborn and God
> Himself – and still get the support of Christian voters. We can not
> allow that to happen. We do not have God's permission to play
> political games with the lives of His children ... No more wheelin'

and dealin'. No more selling out to politicians who negotiate with America's death merchants ... If we are worthy of calling ourselves Christians and pro-life, we should be strong enough to say that politicians who won't take a stand for life are not morally qualified for public office. A candidate whose position on the murder of unborn children is wrong, cannot be "right enough" on other issues to deserve our support.[11]

As we were coming up to the 1996 presidential elections, I asked Flip about the role of the "pro-life" campaign in choosing a Republican candidate:

What is the role of the pro-life campaign in American politics?

Now the Democrats are pro-abortion there's no question about it. But the Republicans are trying to be a big tent, you know, we've got room for this and that ... trying to be very pluralistic and the answer is, it isn't going to happen. In much the same way the Whig party fell apart back in 1857 and a new party was founded. The democrats were pro-slavery, they called it pro-choice back then in the slavery days. And then the Whig party just tried to be a big tent and what happened [was that] there was a new party formed. They nominated as their first Presidential candidate Abraham Lincoln. Of course that was the founding of the Grand Old Party – the Republican party. And our Republican party is facing this same thing and the question is "Is it going to just totally come apart, or is it going to be a party of principle?" Once again I think the answer is it's going to come totally apart. I just think that that's what's going to happen because if they give us a [Republican nominee of] [Robert] Dole, a [Phil] Graham, or a Colin Powell, I mean there will be a mass exodus of Christian votes. We will not any longer vote for a person who is not principally pro-life, who is not principally in the world view which is the seed of the woman.

The Republican party is doing its very best to stay together. I understand they are looking for somebody that will save them because they see this huge rift that is coming which may even, and I think this will be a travesty, but it may allow another four years of Mr Clinton, which would be devastating. But we will not compromise on this issue any more. It would be devastating [but] the fact of the matter is this is a Gospel issue. We are going to stand where the world [our world view] would have us stand. We win the battle on the streets. There are fewer abortions today than there were in 1976. Also in 1986, only 11 percent of the medical training facilities teach the procedure – it's down from 56 percent in 1975. The abortionists are getting gray – they call it "the graying of the abortion industry." They are all older doctors and none of the young doctors want to be an abortionist. You know, I mean it just ruins your practice. There's such a stigma about being an abortionist. So the battle is being won on the streets, not politically.

We [pro-life supporters] are not a real legislative people, all of us are priests and churchmen. We know that where "the rubber meets the road" is in direct action – when you actually and directly intervene as Jesus had to. In order to save us, he had to directly intervene on our behalf. So we are called on directly to intervene and then follow the politics … But we have confronted them [politicians] with the fact that Jesus is the center, that we're *pro-life*. It says on the back, "Without exception, Without compromise and Without apology." But if you are not going to stand here, you're not going to stand on anything else for us, because you are not going to get our vote. [We] just confront the Republican party, which is our party for the most part. Confront them with the truth – that you must take this principle stand here. Stop [being] the politician and politics, which is the art of compromise, and become a statesman, which is the art of principle … You are going to see in time that there are statesmen [who agree with this principle]. But the media is totally ignoring them. They are in the back and God is raising them up. They're coming to fight this goal and you'll see new leadership in the United States of America like you have never seen before. And you'll wonder where did they come from all of a sudden. [But] it isn't so much all of a sudden … God has been preparing these people for these positions.

The problem is the media. Most of the media and politicians do not understand the religious experience. They don't understand what would cause people, without making any money [or] wanting any position, to stand and be so recalcitrant in the face of so many things that are coming against them.

What does the future look like?

The battle between the two seeds that's going on right now, these two world views that are clashing into one another – like a warm front and a cold front – is always going to bring with it great turmoil. There is turmoil in America and there is huge turmoil in the Republican party. I know that the folks in Britain don't have any idea about what's really happening here – that there is a people that serve another camp called Jesus and they will not back off. Of course that was what John Wesley brought over to this land and we are standing on it. Of course unfortunately the Methodist Church has forgotten much of her heritage. Well I'm a Methodist minister too, and I really don't have a place in that church … you know, by and large they're pro-abortion.

Just remember the seed of the serpent and the seed of the woman. Just remember that the more and more liberal you are, the more and more it's "my rights, my body, my choice, my ... " It's why the homosexual community is always around the abortion mill. You often wonder why are they out there being escorts ... and helping these people, making all sorts of noise so that the lady can never hear [us]. They'll scream at the top of their lungs so that they can't hear us whilst we are giving them the Gospel message ... Why would the homosexual community be at the abortion mill? What do they care about reproductive rights? The fact is they understand the battle that is in the Church of Jesus Christ. This is a battle, over whose laws reign. Is it "my rights, my body, my choice" or is it "not my will but thine will be done?" You see abortion is just a symptom of this huge battle over who is king, whose laws are going to reign. But understand, they [homosexuals] understand the battle. They see better than we do. They know that "my rights, my body, my choice" that a woman exercises when she goes in there, is the same thing that they are demanding. It's "my rights, my body, my choice" – I do whatever I want to do behind closed doors and you don't have any right to say anything about me. [They will argue that] as a matter of fact I am a homosexual by gender and therefore I reserve all of the rights as any Black person, I am just a little different. The question is, "Were you born that way or were you not?" You see, the alcoholic, was he born that way or was he not? God calls it a sin. Now everybody is born with an adulterous nature, does that mean you have to live it out – I mean does that mean you have to be like any barnyard dog? God says no. He calls it sin and he calls homosexuality sin and he calls killing his children a sin.

MISS NORMA, MISS NORMA ...

The final character caught up in this drama is Norma McCorvey, "Jane Roe." Her reflections about the case can be found in her book, *I am Roe*.[12] Although I did not speak with her, the pictures painted of her by both Benham and Weddington are, to say the least, confusing. The basic story is that of a young, single woman who was pregnant with her second child in 1972 and wanted to have an abortion in a state where that was illegal. She approached someone in Dallas who she thought could give her information about obtaining an illegal abortion. This person then put her in contact with Sarah Weddington and Linda Coffee, two young lawyers who he knew were looking for a case to challenge the anti-abortion laws. Beyond those facts reigns confusion. For example, it is unclear, either from Weddington's notes or from Benham's comments, as to whether McCorvey knew she would not be able to get an abortion when agreeing to challenge this law. Benham maintains that Norma thought Weddington would get her an abortion. Weddington says that McCorvey was made aware that the legal procedure would be lengthy and that even if the case was won, it would be too late for her to have an abortion. In the book, Norma herself writes of the shock upon realizing the case would be decided after she had the baby. But the story in the book is very different from Norma's story today. For example, we can be certain that by writing *I am Roe*, by signing the movie contract for *Roe* v. *Wade*, by campaigning for pro-choice, and by working at an abortion clinic, Norma was, at some stage, proud of her part in the pro-choice movement. However, in 1995 Norma became an employee of Operation Rescue. So it is equally clear that she has had a change of mind, and heart, about her role. Before we examine all of this more closely, let's listen to Norma's story as found in *I am Roe*:

In February 1970 I was Norma McCorvey, a pregnant street person. A twenty-one-year-old woman in big trouble. I became Jane Roe at a corner table at Colombo's, an Italian restaurant at Mockingbird Lane and Greenville Avenue, in Dallas. I'd suggested to Linda Coffee that we meet there ...

Linda Coffee and Sarah Weddington, sitting together, stood out in Colombo's. Both were older than me, and both were wearing two-piece business suits. Nice clothing, expensive looking. One of them was tall and dark and thin. Delicate. The other was short and blond and a little plump, her hair in a stiff-looking permanent ...

I was wearing jeans, a button-down shirt tied at the waist, and sandals. I wore my bandanna tied around my left leg, above the knee. That meant I didn't have a girlfriend.

I walked over to their table. It was obvious to me even from across the room that these women hadn't talked to a person like me for a long time, if ever ...

"Hi. I'm Norma McCorvey?" I said. The shorter blond woman

came to life. "I'm Sarah Weddington," she said. Sarah Weddington reached out and shook my hand. Linda introduced herself, too, but it was apparent right away that Sarah was the one who would speak for both of them ... [13]

... I was six months pregnant by the time the trial was over. When I called in, Linda told me to come right over. She sounded excited. After I finally arrived, hot and tired, she said that she had both good news and bad news to tell me. The good news was that we had won the case ... The bad news was that I had lost ... Wade had announced he would appeal the case ... and prosecute any doctor who performed an abortion on a woman. "Well, then, Linda, how long will the appeal take?" I asked. "A while," she said. "But, Norma, what does it matter? An abortion has to be performed in the first twenty-four weeks of pregnancy, and it's clearly too late for you now."

The world stopped ... I had a moment of clarity ... This lawsuit was not really for me. It was about me, and maybe all the women who'd come before me, but it was really for all the women who were coming after me. I would have to have my baby after all ... [14]

... "Feeding time!" she said. "What?" "Feeding time!" she said, again. Then she handed me the baby. I can't tell you all the horrible feelings that went through me at that moment. It was like getting a glimpse of hell – all my shame and fear and guilt and love and sadness all rolled up into a ball and placed in front of me.

Was this my baby? Why were they giving it to me? Should I look at it? Or not look at it? ...

There was flap of cloth over its face. My entire body, my entire soul cried out to me to turn the flap down, to look at my baby's face. But my mind told me that it would be the worst thing I could ever do ... My mind won. My heart lost. I never touched the flap. I felt sick to my stomach. I start crying, loudly, in pure despair ... [15]

This despair ultimately led Norma to attempt suicide. But throughout the book, she maintains a strong pro-choice position. The final paragraph leaves no doubt about her beliefs: "People of all nations who are pro-choice and pro-family, stand up and be counted. Support pro-choice candidates who are running for office. Write your state legislators and congressmen and congresswomen ... Let the US Supreme Court and our government hear our voices: Silence no more! We will not go back!"[16]

Another bit of confusion surrounds Norma's sexuality. In the book, she confirms that she has been in a lesbian relationship for a number of years with "Connie." Since her conversion to Christianity, Benham has argued that while she has been a lesbian, Connie and Norma are now only "roommates." One article summarizes Benham's understanding of her sexuality: "Much has been made about her lesbian relationship. Mr Benham says to give her time. He says that Miss McCorvey's relationship with 'Miss Connie' ... who kept her alive through overdoses and drunkenness ... is basically for all intents and purposes simply a strong friendship between roommates now; there has been no lesbian sex for years, he says. And, insists Mr Benham, 'Miss Connie wants to meet the Lord'."[17] It remains uncertain how Norma would describe her sexuality at present.

Unable to speak with her myself, I am left with a rather blurred understanding of Norma's story. While the book offers one picture, it certainly does not match that of the new Norma. So I asked Sarah and Flip about Norma's role in the case and subsequent events. Needless to say, they offer very different accounts:

Sarah, can you tell me about Norma McCorvey: about your first meeting and her recent change of position?

She has actually had a book come out in the last couple of years called *I am Roe*. So she documents things that I can now say which I couldn't before because of [confidentiality]. She ran away from home the first time at 11; was in a reformatory school by 13; had trouble with alcohol, trouble with drugs; sold drugs for a period; has now had three children – but raised none of them. The first one her mother took away, on the basis that she was unfit to raise a child. [She] never finished high school. It was a fairly unstable life for her. The original deal with Jane Roe was that it would cost her nothing. That she could be anonymous and that it would take not much time. So she did sign the one page legal affidavit. In terms of the original part of the case we never expected that she would ever be public. I don't know that she thought about it in great detail, but certainly that was the understanding when we went into it. I don't know that she thought about the issue public versus non-public. But you see, even when she sold her story for the movie – and she was the one who initiated that, I was not in favor of it – they gave her the choice of using her real name or not and she choice to use her false name. So she didn't use her real name even though everybody else did. During the time of the case she moved frequently, so it was hard to be able to call her and keep her as informed as we would have liked. So she learned, according to the story, through the newspaper and that may be accurate. The woman with her in the movie is Connie, who has been her lover for many years now. I haven't talked to her personally. So what I know [about her joining Operation Rescue] is what I have seen in the press. And in the press it seems that her position is not [very clear] because she is saying [that] she is still for abortion in the first trimester, which is certainly not the position of the group she is working with. So I have heard her say a number of things, I don't know what her position is today. I do know from a legal perspective it doesn't matter, it's a class action. I wish she had not changed. I think it does give the opposition ammunition but it doesn't chip at the underpinnings of the case or anything like that. The person who converted her and then held the baptism in the backyard swimming pool with ABC News present is the same guy that Planned Parenthood of Houston got a judgment against for illegal activity during the last Republican convention, the national Republican convention, in Houston. Then a doctor recently in Dallas won a judgment of something like $8 million for harassment and other activities. The same Flip Benham is one of those against whom that judgment was entered.

Flip, how do you understand Norma's role in *Roe* v. *Wade*?

Norma said that she had been raped to Sarah Weddington, who was an attorney and Linda Coffee who was an attorney, who were looking for a class action suit so that they could legalize abortion – that every woman would have a right to choose whether or not to kill her child, given a choice. So 25 years ago it began right here in a little pizza parlor on Greenville Avenue. And then Norma said "O.K. I'll be that person that you can use to go ahead and work this class action suit." Of course Norma thought that she was going to be able to get an abortion, [that] Sarah Weddington would help her get an abortion. Sarah Weddington had no intention of doing that and she didn't. Norma did not abort that baby and so it began here. It was a suit that was filed against "Jane Roe," that was Norma's name [pseudonym], and Henry Wade who was the District Attorney in the city of Dallas and it made its long ugly journey up to the Supreme Court. Supreme Court ruled on January 22nd 1973. Now it has come full circle right back to Dallas – to the very lady who was used to do this. She's now saying I will do everything I can to undo what was done. So it's been an interesting circle.

Norma will come out and speak with us and she's a professing, confessing Christian. She is 100 percent pro-life. The lady whose name they used to bring this whole nasty thing in, who just weeps when she sees an empty playground and realizes that there are kids that could have been [playing there] but are not there because of something that [she] helped to do. It's pretty interesting that Jane Roe, who was used to usher in this horrible thing, never had an abortion. She is a professing, confessing Christian. You see the tables are turning here in America, even though the laws aren't. The laws ... they'll catch up with us in about ten years. Right now everything is getting turned upside down and the abortion industry knows it. They are on the downward side of a slippery slope.

What do you think people believe about Norma McCorvey joining your campaign?

The fact of the matter is that this is what being a Christian is all about. They don't understand, they don't comprehend it. When Norma got baptized and Peter Jennings [news reader] of ABC News said "Well, this marks a huge political shift for Miss McCorvey from Pro-choice to Pro-life." And Peggy Wainmire, who's the lady who did the story down here, who's a born again Christian I understand, said "Mr Jennings you have to understand something here. The film footage we have is of Norma kneeling in front of empty swings in a playground and weeping and her being baptized in the pool. This isn't a political shift, this is far deeper than that and if you are going to run the footage you better say why she was baptized, that means something." Of course that doesn't mean anything to Mr Jennings because he doesn't understand, he doesn't. He doesn't understand what it means to move from the seed of the serpent to the seed of the woman. That's a huge paradigm shift, from one world view to another.

How did Norma McCorvey come to work for Operation Rescue?

She used to work [at the abortion clinic]. She was working right next door. We moved in and *Time Magazine* did a big article on "Roe meets Rescue." Miss Norma said there's going to be violence and tears and Tom Sneider [TV political commentator] interviewed her and he said "Now don't let those b.a.s.t.a.r.d.s wear you down." They were just laughing and Norma said "Oh no, I won't, they're not going to get to me." But the Gospel of Jesus Christ did get to Norma and I got to talk to her. I remember one day coming out here and it was Saturday morning and I said "Miss Norma, Miss Norma what are you going to do?" and she said "I don't

117

know." So we just went over and sat on the park bench which was right here and we talked ... I shared with her the Gospel of Jesus that I know and we struck up quite a friendship, relationship. She really liked [two children of staff at OR] and they had a big part in inviting her to church. Then a newspaper guy came out and got some pictures of Norma and I and [he] said "strange friends – here is the director of Operation Rescue and then this lady who is the pro-choice idol of this nation, and here they are friends, how can that be?" And then ultimately on July 22nd Norma gave her heart to Christ and was a new creation, brand new. Then on August 8th she was baptized and she has been with us ever since. [When she worked at the abortion clinic next door] she would send ladies over here that were going in there. Already there are five folks who used to work there but don't work there anymore. I mean Jesus is just pillaging the abortion industry, saving the folks out of that mess. I mean that's how we win. If you set the goal in the name of Jesus and let him go to work – we don't do a lot, we just show up and we give him an excuse to do "exceedingly, abundantly, above all we ask or imagine," and he does. The business over here [at the clinic next door] has dropped incredibly. They're doing everything they can to just move us out and shut us up. The doctor over there made each and every employee sign a statement that "I will not associate with people in Operation Rescue during work hours." The second part was "I will not associate with people in Operation Rescue after hours: to do so would be considered immoral." He made each one sign, because he knows that if they will associate with us very long there is something that draws them and it isn't us, but it draws them from that over [there] to here. Five of them, and we'd only been here a week. Believe me, many, many, many, many [mothers] have changed their minds because we have given them a real choice outside that door, a choice other than abortion.

Without a doubt, Norma McCorvey has undergone a significant change in the way in which she understands her role in one of the most controversial issues in America. It would be easy to sit in my ivory tower miles away from Norma McCorvey and pass judgment about her. Was she a pawn for Sarah Weddington and Linda Coffee who needed a name in order to challenge anti-abortion laws? Is she a pawn for Flip Benham and Operation Rescue to attract media attention to their pro-life campaign? The only person who can answer those questions is Norma McCorvey. I can, however, empathize with her. And with the many women in the American South who try to make sense out of their lives as they navigate the religious storm over abortion. Many of their stories will never be heard. Fearing judgment, their decision, their abortion, their memories will remain unknown to their families and friends. Their hearts however are the real battlegrounds of the abortion debate. No matter how much a woman knows her rights, no matter how well she knows her reasons, walking into an abortion clinic hearing shouts of "murderer" will always stay with her. Even if she believes, knows, she is not, it is frightening to think there are so many who think she is.

KEY FIGURES IN THE DEBATE

By now you will have noticed that the style in this chapter is different from the rest. The others that I spoke with all told stories that I could more easily work into prose. My choice to leave Sarah and Flip in interview style was to some degree about their positioning to the subject. As key, or leading, figures in the debate they each offer a different perspective that is best left in their own words. They even offer a story about Norma. But that is not the main reason for this style. When writing is difficult it is easier to distance it, to objectify it. This chapter has been the most difficult for me to finish. Unlike the other bits of life I have shared, this particular pool offers a disturbing reflection.

I remember seeing the blue dot. I had been barfing for days. A friend was with me and she said "What are you going to do?" It was 10 p.m., I hadn't waited for the first morning pee. I picked up the phone and called my mom and dad. And told them. No working up to it, just told them. Within half an hour I was on the road home from college. I knew exactly what I was going to do. The distance from Abilene to my parents' home was 300 miles. There was a 60-mile stretch of two lane farm-to-market road that cut through some canyons. It would be after midnight, no traffic. It would look like an accident. This was years before *Thelma & Louise*. No noble ideas, just an easy end to it all. As I approached the turn north through the canyon, two semi-trailers came up behind me. They followed me for a mile after the turn, so I slowed down to let them pass. One sped around. And then, no matter how fast or slow I drove, one stayed behind me and one in front for the next 60 miles. Divine intervention? Maybe. Maybe I decided to make it home.

When I walked through the door, mom and dad hugged me and asked what I wanted. Really. No "What the hell are you going to do now?" No "How could you?" Just simply "What do you want?" I was an "A" student with serious ambition for life. I had fought hard, literally, to get out of a small town with my virginity because I wanted a life. I had never wanted to wake up next to some guy for the rest of my life. And I had been barfing every ten minutes for a solid month. The next day we left for Dallas. To my parents' credit, they were supportive, caring – worried – but loving. I did not speak to them the entire journey. We spent the night in a hotel and arrived early at the clinic. Memories are vague. I don't recall protesters. My mom came in with me initially and when I was called she and dad went across the street to the International House of Pancakes.

There was a counseling session – I barfed the whole time. There was a scan. I was hardly a month along. The nurse said something about possibly having to come back in a few weeks. Eventually they decided I was pregnant enough. A bit of anesthetic. I was awake but felt nothing. On his way out of the room, I asked the doctor a question. I can't remember what. All I recall is him hunching over this jar keeping it out of sight. Obviously unaware that I can't see a thing without my glasses. I never even saw him. After a quick rest, I got dressed, climbed into the backseat of the car and we left Dallas. A little way out of town, they stopped for something to eat. I barfed for the last time. Two days later, back at college, I turned in my ethics paper on abortion.

Ten years later, to the month, I am writing again about abortion. Two thoughts come to mind. What the hell would I do with a ten-year-old? A trailer, a McJob, and a husband – but not a life. The second is even more unsettling. Other than my parents, and a couple of old girlfriends, no one knows this story. And still I worry about what my family, my father's church members, might think. Judgment is easy. Choices are not. Choosing life is different for every person in every situation. We make choices and we live with them. I ain't the only one.

Jill was a medical student, a scientist, and one of my closest friends in college. During one drunken girls' night, I remember her telling us how (scientifically) difficult it was to get pregnant – the small probability, the need for exact timing. I didn't actually believe her until years later when a lesbian friend was going through the insemination process, for months and months. In Jill's final year, after being accepted into an elite medical school, the odds were against her. Should she have a baby now as her dreams were about to be realized? Or should she wait until she was married, out of medical school, and could provide for a child? She and her boyfriend made the same "trip to Dallas." She finished school and now has her own successful medical practice. As well as a husband and children. Jill chose life. Her life.

Jane and I were never friends. We had grown up together, both preachers' daughters, went to church camp together, went to the same college. But never friends. Her father, and therefore Jane, was a pew jumper – a right-wing Christian evangelist. She showed up at my dorm room one night in tears. She had gotten pregnant, went home, had an abortion, returned to school and was promptly dumped by her long-time boyfriend. She needed to talk to another preacher's daughter – not about Christian forgiveness. My reputation was, well, a little less saintly than hers. Even though unknown to her, I was still a virgin. Assuming my reputation was all true, she hoped for an understanding ear. While recovering from her visit to the clinic, Jane was resting on the living room couch reading a romance novel. One of those with a title like *Summer of Love*. Her father walked in, looked at the book, and said, "We all know where a summer of love has gotten you." Judgment from a preacher is damning enough. Judgment from a preacher who is also "daddy" is hell. The last time I bumped into Jane she was at a revival with her parents. I don't know if Jane chose life. I don't know who chose. I don't know what kind of life.

Sometimes choices are informed – by science, by ideology, by religion. Sometimes they just come from the gut. Preparing for my ethics assignment ten years ago I did not read feminist theories on abortion. A brief synopsis of the case and a couple of articles from old, male theologians were plenty for a short essay. Now Flip's words remind me of Rosalind Petchesky's commentary on a women's right to choose in her book *Abortion and Woman's Choice*:

> The idea that "my body belongs to me" ... expresses the value of self-determination, but it transcends the negative, exclusionary connotation of bourgeois individualism which often associates it with property rights. It asserts that people's need for autonomy in the decisions that affect their bodies, their persons, is an indispensable condition of their full participation in society. This is the underlying principle of a feminist morality of abortion. It protests the deep contradiction in "pro-life" ideology – and Christian patriarchy – which treats women's bodies as passive vessels yet holds women morally responsible for what becomes of fetuses, and children.[18]

My body belongs to me. For Flip, what a sacrilege. For so many others, what a revolutionary thought. Many times I have questioned the apparent mission of the church: judging individuals as they grapple with the complexity of life. My theology is a bit rusty. However, I do recall one fundamental commandment: "To love your neighbor as yourself" (Matthew 22:39). Do this and you shall live.

NOTES

1 A number of groups filed *amicus curiae* briefs in support of Weddington's argument, including the American Jewish Congress, the Episcopal Diocese of New York, the Union of Hebrew Congregations, Unitarians, the United Church of Christ, and the Board of Christian Social Concerns of the United Methodist Church.

2 V. Samar, *The Right to Privacy* (Philadelphia: Temple University Press, 1991), p. 34.

3 S. Weddington, *A Question of Choice* (New York: Penguin, 1992), p. 118.

4 All quotations in this paragraph are taken from *Roe* v. *Wade* 410 US 113, majority decision.

5 *Ibid.*

6 S. Weddington, *A Question of Choice*.

7 *Ibid.*, p. 11.

8 *Ibid.*, p. 149.

9 F. Benham, "The Way of the Cross: No Cheap Solutions" (Dallas, TX: Operation Rescue).

10 J. B. Pack, "Abortion: The Black Woman's Voice" (Jefferson City, MO: Easton Publishing Company, Inc., 1995).

11 "Jesus is the Standard" (Dallas, TX: Operation Rescue).

12 N. McCorvey with A. Meisler, *I Am Roe: My Life, Roe v. Wade, and Freedom of Choice* (New York: HarperCollins, 1994).

13 *Ibid.*, pp. 117–18.

14 *Ibid.*, pp. 126–7.

15 *Ibid.*, p. 131.

16 *Ibid.*, p. 209.

17 J. Maxwell, "Driving Miss Norma," *World Magazine* (Asheville, N.C.: God's World Publications Inc., August 26/September 2, 1995), p. 16.

18 R. Petchesky, *Abortion and Woman's Choice: The State, Sexuality and Reproductive Freedom* (London: Verso, 1986), extract courtesy of M. Humm (ed.), *Feminisms* (London: Harvester Wheatsheaf, 1992), pp. 293–4.

Chapter Five

CONDITIONAL LOVE

*If a man lies with a male as with a woman, both of them have
committed an abomination; they shall be put to death.*

(Leviticus 20:13)

*If I speak in the tongues of men and of angels, but have not love, I am
a noisy gong or a clanging cymbal. And if I have prophetic powers,
and understand all mysteries and all knowledge, and if I have all
faith, so as to remove mountains, but have not love, I am nothing.*

(1 Corinthians 13:1–2)

*Though not direct or overt, heterosexism is a form of discrimination.
Its subtlety makes it somehow even more insidious because it is harder
to combine and combat. Heterosexism is discrimination by neglect,
omission, and/or distortion, whereas often its more active partner –
homophobia – is discrimination by intent and design.*[1]

The debate about one's ability to choose figures highly in the
debate over homosexuality. Perceived as a choice, homosexuality as
sin threatens the individual's soul as well as the collective values of
Southern Christian society. As such, homosexuals should be saved,
but more importantly, society should not be fooled: "We are facing
the Devil himself in these homosexuals."[2] However, similar to the
variety of Christian positions on abortion, homosexuality and
Christianity are not mutually exclusive. Indeed for those of us, gay
men and lesbians, who grew up in the Bible Belt, they are probably
the two most influential aspects of our social and personal psyche.
This chapter begins by highlighting the beliefs of the Christian
Right, and their manifestations in the Bible Belt. But the story
doesn't end there. The second section offers stories of gay men and

lesbians who have had various experiences at the hands of such "good Christians." Hatred sometimes breeds hatred, and a number of them feel nothing but contempt for those who systematically marginalize and abuse them. Alternatively, some have hung on to their own Christian beliefs, translating them into a doctrine of God's unconditional love.

Before I head down this particular road, allow me to tell you a bit more about my own history with Southern Christianity. At the age of 17 I was president of Methodist Youth in seven states. I was heavily involved in organizing spiritual conferences – liaising with speakers, Christian music groups, budgeting, etc. – as well as legislative conferences where church policy on youth ministry was determined. I won't bore you with too many details but a few are unavoidable. In America, the hierarchy of the United Methodist Church is similar to a representational democracy. Each level – local, district, conference, jurisdictional, and general – has various committees dealing with various tasks, for example educational, missionary, and administrative. And each committee usually has a "youth representative." As jurisdictional president, I spent as much time sitting on these committees as I did in a high school classroom. They were every bit as much a learning experience. I have no doubt my love of, and cynicism about, politics started whilst I watched good Christian men battle for positions of power. So, my experience of the church from an early age was rather different than that of the average member sitting in the same pew for 30 years.

By the time I headed off to a Methodist university, I had preached sermons to congregations of over 3,000. During college I worked for four years as a paid youth minister and afterwards for one year as a lay pastor. Many expected me to continue my studies at seminary. Graduate school did build upon what I had learned – not theology but politics. While there are many incidents that led to my chosen path, the most significant was coming out. Quite simply, there was no place in the church for a lesbian. The church made this message fairly clear. For example, I recall one bishop's sermon to a packed sanctuary of Methodist ministers. His two points caused two very different responses from the congregation: the first, something about church unity, got the usual yawns and glazed looks; the second, that he would never ordain a homosexual as a preacher, got a standing ovation. Since then it has never ceased to amaze me how efficiently a common enemy can build unity.

Hoping things had changed, I headed for Nashville, headquarters of Methodism, to visit with a national youth minister. She informed me that the general conference, the national legislative body, had just recently discussed the church's position on homosexuality. Likewise, the national youth legislative body had held a similar debate. During this debate, many Southern youth leaders had forced their youth delegates to leave the hall – arguing that discussing homosexuality would lead them away from the Lord. One 35-year-old Southern male youth minister expressed his good Christian beliefs, as well as his youth work skills, by yelling abuse at the 18-year-old chairperson. So although Methodism is seen as a fairly liberal, or at least a socially conscious denomination, there remains a substantial voice in Southern Methodism which continues to reject gay men and lesbians as part of the church. And this homophobic position wields a substantial amount of power. For example, general council employees have to sign a certificate of compliance stating that Methodist funds have not been used to promote homosexuality. Apparently, it is a more appropriate use of funds to promote rejection. For those of us who grew up in the church, there is nothing more personally frightening than rejection and damnation to hell. It has taken me a while to learn that no matter who yells, or how loud, the whereabouts of my soul in the afterlife is not up to them.

CHRISTIAN VALUES

Of course that lesson is not an easy one to learn, especially when it feels the whole world believes you are going to hell and so deserve whatever happens on earth. Some remember where they were when Kennedy, or Elvis, or Diana, died. I remember exactly where I was when I first heard of AIDS – sitting in a pew in First Methodist Church, Abilene, Texas. Unbeknownst to me, a magazine had just

printed an article about a bishop who had died of AIDS, claiming
that he had not caught HIV from ministering to victims of the
disease, as his family had announced, but that he in fact had been a
gay man and had caught the disease from a clandestine encounter.
The local preacher was livid. He knew the bishop, had been friends
with him, and knew he was not a "homo-sex-u-al." He was a man of
God, and was in heaven. Homosexuals were going to hell, particularly those that did not learn from this Godly plague and turn from
their sinful ways. At the beginning of the AIDS crisis in the early
1980s, as the gay community suffered and died, good Christian
nations, who had previously believed science and medicine would
eventually cure other diseases, seemed happy to believe this one was
sent by God.

While, years later, many have returned to faith in medicine, many
in the rural South continue to believe that AIDS is inextricably, if
not causally, linked to homosexuality. Driving into a small Southern city (population approximately 100,000), I decided to stop by an
AIDS support project to see what attitudes were like in the late
1990s. A senior worker, a local man in his late fifties, happily
informed me of the "great" educational program – one staff
member who, when invited, led seminars on HIV. "She started out
the first couple of years concentrating on schools and educating the
public. But her job description was changed and now she works
only with high risk groups." When I asked him to identify those
high-risk communities he shrugged, "jails, drug users, ethnic minorities ... we don't really have a large visible community to work
outreach." To me, there was an obvious omission so, after he noted
that there were 75 cases of AIDS in the local area, I asked about
their identity. "There's about seven or eight women, ten heterosexuals [*sic*] and the rest would be gay." He quickly added that this
organization had nothing to do with gay rights. "The group is
committed to the fight against AIDS. This group is not pro-gay or
anti-gay. Our mission is not about being gay." He was desperate to
disassociate the support agency from the gay community, even
though most of the volunteers were gay men and lesbians and most
of those suffering from AIDS in the vicinity were gay men.

His point became a bit more clear after I heard tales of how their financial and medical support depended on extremely tenuous local support. While the – as in the *only* – local gay bar had a few fundraisers for the agency, most of their financial support came from very public charity events – in respectable straight society.

> We have had a fashion show, a "Truman Capote black and white" party at the Center for Contemporary Arts ... We've learned to do what we can in the community. We've learned to be aggressive and yet to try and be visible in "different" ways that would have a positive community impact, instead of exciting the community in a negative way against us.

This public face has to be careful how it presents itself. For example, the agency had applied to have a float in the annual veterans' day parade and were denied because the organizers did not want "gay militants" on their fine city streets. "They were fearful of some from the gay community being very visible in that parade." Even medical assistance is conditional and subject to moral and social regulation. For a number of years the city had only one doctor who would provide health care for HIV/AIDS patients. Recently he left the area. Now a doctor from Dallas flies in once a month to provide care. The only additional medical help is provided by a rural doctor who drives in once a month. However, fearing he will lose his small practice if anyone finds out, he offers assistance on the condition that he remains anonymous.

Distancing itself from the gay community in order to secure "benefits" is perhaps somewhat understandable. In most of the Bible Belt, homosexuality is a crime – hatred expressed towards them is not. In late December 1997, the one gay and lesbian bar in the town was burnt to the ground. While the arson made headlines in the local paper, the text never noted that it was a gay bar nor mentioned the words "hate crime." Revisiting the area I passed by the remains of the building and could clearly see "faggots" spray-painted on the rubble. Urban, dare I say Yankee, AIDS activism raises awareness with the slogan SILENCE = DEATH. And for those in this local gay community, where HIV education is given to everyone but them, silence has certainly led to death. But silence has also been the price they pay to get any help, financial or medical. It is the same across the rural South for many gay men and lesbians – silence may be their only hope for life.

Social marginalization and victimization of gay men and lesbians rarely makes for news in the Bible Belt. A recent cover story for *Newsweek* addressed the backlash against gay men and lesbians felt across America.[3] It cited two incidents in the South: "Irmo High School in South Carolina barred the lesbian folk-rock duo Indigo Girls from performing on campus" and "Ross Perot [the former independent presidential candidate] revoked domestic-partnership benefits at his Dallas computer-services company."[4] In May 1996, Cobb County, Georgia refused to repeal their anti-gay ordinance as requested by the Olympic committee who had planned for the Olympic torch to travel through the county.[5] In the South such fervent beliefs are echoed by all those wishing to "cleanse" society. For example, in August 1987 KKK demonstrators in a Cumming, Georgia parade wore T-shirts proclaiming "Thank God for AIDS."[6]

Now of course not every member of the Christian Right is a member of the KKK. But my point here is that the effects of their shared agenda of hate are the same. While the Christian Right has failed to have abortion laws repealed, their highly organized network has been directed firmly at homosexuals. In June 1996 the Southern Baptist Convention, representing 16 million members, voted to boycott the Disney Corporation because it recognized same-sex partners of employees for insurance benefits; hosted homosexual and lesbian theme nights at its parks; and was associated with the publication of a book entitled *Growing Up Gay*.[7] In October 1996 the *Texas Triangle*, a gay and lesbian newspaper, went out of business due, in part, to the efforts of the Texas chapter of the American Family Association which "helped orchestrate an advertiser boycott" leading to "one less homosexual newspaper espousing the virtues of the sinful lifestyle."[8]

The AFA is a "Christian organization promoting the Biblical

ethic of decency in American society with primary emphasis on TV and other media."[9] It is one of many similar organizations on the Christian Right which believes homosexuals are a threat to society. In order to present their argument clearly, I have chosen below a excerpt from a recent AFA article, "Homosexuality in America: Exposing the Myths."[10] While not every Southern Christian is a member of the AFA, I can personally testify that these beliefs are held by many in the Bible Belt. Hell, I'm kinned to a few:

Myth #8 Homosexuals are an oppressed minority and should have the same civil rights extended to them regarding their homosexuality as other minorities ... There are several things wrong with regarding homosexuality as a civil right. First the law already protects the civil rights of citizens. Homosexuals now enjoy these civil rights as everyone else does ... To extend protection to a homosexual on the basis of his homosexuality is unnecessary and unfair. One's behavior should not be the subject of civil rights laws ... Second, homosexuality is not a benign factor like race ... No one is interested in the observation that Blacks tend to have darker skin than whites. This trivial observation is irrelevant to any debate concerning race. However, the claim that all Blacks are lazy is an irrational racist belief because there is no connection between a person's laziness and his race. When it comes to the behavior of homosexuals that is relevant to the debate about homosexuality. Why would anyone oppose someone's homosexuality? Precisely because of their homosexuality ... It is not irrational for one to oppose homosexuality, since the factor that one opposes is related to the homosexuals as homosexuals ... Third, the criteria to judge whether or not a group is an oppressed minority do not apply to the homosexual community ... There must be a history of discrimination evidenced by the lack of ability to obtain economic mean income, adequate education or cultural opportunity ... Protected classes should exhibit obvious, immutable, or distinguishing characteristics, like race, color, gender, that define them as a discrete group ... There is no reason to regard homosexuals as an oppressed minority.

Myth #9 Homosexuals are normal, healthy, everyday people ... There can be no doubt that most Americans would be repulsed if they could see the decadence within the homosexual community ...

> Despite what homosexual advocates would like us to believe, testimony from those who have come out of the homosexual lifestyle as well as video accounts of events such as gay rights parades evidence the fact that the homosexual lifestyle is characterized by anonymous sexual encounters and celebration of sexual obsession and perversion unparalleled in any other social group ... Are homosexuals as healthy as everyone else? ... Less than 2% of homosexuals survive to 65. This statistic is so extreme, no doubt because of the disparate percentage of homosexuals with AIDS, as compared to the rest of society ...[11]

The article concludes that the appropriate Christian response is to "forestall the further advance of the homosexual agenda" and to "be willing to help the recovering homosexual grow in his relationship with Christ."[12] Having read this, and being familiar with similar arguments, I believe we can locate the foundation of these beliefs on the notion of choice. The Christian Right maintains that homosexuality is a choice of sexual behavior. And that such a choice is sin. As a child of a nation where religious freedom is paramount, I have no quarrel with this belief. I don't happen to share it, but I ain't got no right to tell them what to believe. And vice versa.

I do think it is worth drawing some parallels between this conception of homosexuality and their beliefs about abortion. First, both are seen as sinful choices. Second, because they are sinful, the state should not allow such behavior. There should be laws against abortion and laws against homosexuality. Now while I can applaud their desire to have laws reflect a moral standard, I'm not quite sure that every possible sin should be regulated by the state. Surely that would call into question the whole notion of freedom upon which America was founded.[13]

The article makes a couple of other points that may be worth noting before we consider the lives of gay men and lesbians in the South. First, that "homosexuals" have the same rights as "heterosexuals." And in turn they should not be able to claim that they are discriminated against. Given that the majority of Southern states have sodomy laws, if not more general "anti-gay" legislation, gay men and lesbians do not have the same right as heterosexuals to make choices about their sexual relationships. This lack of rights, if not state-condoned discrimination, does make gay men and lesbians rather socially and politically powerless. For example, the author refers to the income levels of "homosexuals" as being higher than "heterosexuals." While that may, or may not, be true, gay men or lesbians do not have job security.[14] There are no federal laws protecting them from being fired simply because they are gay men or lesbians. Picking up on the comparison with choice about abortion, the same logic would allow someone to be fired because they had an abortion.

Second, most of the article attempts to paint a picture of "homosexual lifestyle" which is "repulsive." This is done in two ways: by noting that it is unhealthy and sexually promiscuous. The examples invoked for proving it is unhealthy refer to AIDS, murder, and suicide. As a communicable disease, HIV/AIDS does not discriminate between heterosexual and homosexual. Unlike the days of the Old Testament, those contracting diseases should receive care rather than condemnation or social exclusion. Similarly, in a society that incites hatred towards gay men and lesbians it is no wonder that more of them are killed or commit suicide. Surely one way to avoid this is to work toward a society that does not condone such hatred.

The "repulsiveness" of homosexuality, we are told, can be seen in any gay pride parade. Now on this point, I do have some sympathy. My nice preacher's daughter sensibilities sometimes have been likewise offended. The difference, however, is that I know that what I see "on parade" doesn't represent every gay man and lesbian. Assuming all gay men and lesbians wear leather etc. is, to use the article's analogy, just like assuming because I see one Black person sitting on a park bench during the day, all Black people are lazy. Many gay men and lesbians do not identify with the images they see at such events. I was speaking to an older lesbian living quietly in the rural South who made that very point: "Being gay is not like all this crap you see on TV or read in papers. We don't wear black leather and the chains. We're not into that stuff."

Having heard the kind of argument made by the Christian Right, I was curious about its impact on young Southern Christians. So I welcomed the opportunity to speak at a large Church of Christ university in the Bible Belt with a class training in "adolescent ministry." At the beginning of the lecture, I asked them to individually define a few terms that I would be using, such as "justice," "equal opportunities" and "freedom." I also asked them to define "sexuality" and write down what they thought a gay man or lesbian looked like. The results were hardly surprising: well over half of the university students believed the stereotypes. Gay men were described as: "girly"; "skinny little things"; "wore earrings"; "pale, skinny frail men"; "more feminine that heterosexuals"; "effeminate mannerisms and voice"; "squirrely looking with long hair on top with pleated pants and funny voice"; "some clean cut good looking men – others dirty looking"; "downplays heterosexual traits"; "effeminate with short hair." Lesbians were described as: "boyish like, unfeminine, stocky stature"; "short hair, don't wear make-up"; "aggressive, assertive, issue driven"; "uncomfortable with femininity"; "strong feminist"; "dresses closer to a male"; "manly, takes on a man's role, dresses in more manly clothes or something neutral, mostly dark colors." While a few did state that homosexuals look "no different" from heterosexuals, several added comments such as: "they look like anyone else but have a problem with sin," "looks like God's creation ... two eyes, two ears, legs, etc ... but marred by a wrong choice of lifestyle that goes against God's word."

I agreed to speak to the class because I was doing this research. The teacher's reason for inviting me was a bit more dubious. According to him, they had never seen, much less spoken to, a lesbian before. While I hope my lecture did not fall on completely deaf ears, the ten minutes of question time began with one student pulling out his Bible, slamming it on the table, and reading to me from Leviticus. Like I ain't heard that one before. I'm afraid the only ground upon which the class and I unanimously could agree was that homosexuals should not be shot. If this class is anything to go by, stereotypes, and the accompanying hatred, appear to be the mantra of the next generation of Southern Christians.

How do these "Christian" values affect the lives of others? Quite frankly, the combination of this Christianity, Southern gendered culture, and KKK militancy makes the Bible Belt a living hell for many gay men and lesbians. Now living in cities across America, those demonized by rural Southern morality have told their stories of physical and psychological suffering. For example, in James Sears' recent book *Growing up Gay in the South,* numerous young people tell of physical violence.[15] Throughout his childhood "Alston" endured "verbal and physical harassment from his fellow students":

> If there had not been such a taboo on being gay or being feminine; if people had not ridiculed me for it as much, it would have been a lot easier ... The thing that was so hard and painful to deal with was all the name calling, the snickers and the laughs, the elbows in the side, knocking my books down or snatching them and throwing them in the garbage. That's what hurt.[16]

In Southern Louisiana in a roadside diner, I sat across from Jen as she recounted her experiences of homophobia: "I have been fired because I was gay. I have been shot at because I was gay. I have been beaten up because I was gay. I have been kicked out of my house because I was gay." In a bar in Nashville, Tony confided that when his father found out he was gay he literally kicked him out of the house. While Tony lay battered and bruised on the front lawn, his father slammed the door yelling, "I didn't raise you to be a sissy!" In Atlanta, Joel recalled the "daily beatings after school." Every bar owner told of regular gay bashings in the parking lot as customers returned to their cars. And most hated calling the police. It would take hours for anyone to arrive, and by then word spread amongst the crowd that cops were on their way. Fearing arrest, or being spotted in a gay bar, patrons quickly vacated the premises. One owner told of a burly policeman who walked in, looked at the beaten customer and simply said, "Well, you deserved that, didn't you, boy?"

For gay men and lesbians who actively choose to live in small Southern towns, the rural idyll can be an isolating nightmare. In Ovett, Mississippi, Brenda and Wanda Henson created a women's retreat and education center, Camp Sister Spirit. The women living and visiting there have been shot at; their dog shot and placed on their mailbox; nails placed systematically on their road; shopkeepers refused to sell to them or charged twice the regular price. Bomb threats and death threats have become a common occurrence. In a neighboring town, one local summed up the motivation behind the harassment: "They're Baptist."[17] Wanda Henson grew up in Mississippi and simply wanted to live a country life and provide a peaceful place of retreat for women. But as any small-town lesbian can testify, being a publicly, or worse politically, out lesbian will always lead to harassment and often to violence.

So again, to live somewhere peacefully in the country necessitates keeping quiet. On my travels I came across lesbians who have chosen to remain in their rural hometown and feel that silence is a small price to pay for family security and familiarity of surroundings.[18] For example, one couple simply don't see the point in causing a fuss. "I'm not the open type. I've got my family to think about, my friends. People are cruel. All you're asking for is trouble, and not only for yourself but for your family too." For a couple of reasons I think it may be easier for lesbians to choose to remain in their hometowns. First, family and friends are likely to see them as one of their own rather than as a threat – either from the outside such as those in Ovett; or because fears about homosexuality are most often directed at gay men. Second, it is more difficult for a single woman to survive economically in the city – women continue to earn less than men. Silence, then, may seem a small price to pay when the alternative is loneliness and financial hardship.

Nevertheless, one thing is clear, gay men and lesbians who grow up in the rural South – where every Sunday Christianity tells all their neighbors that homosexuals are the devil incarnate and should be stopped – either get beaten into silence or leave. Lubbock, Texas often looks best through the the rear-view mirror. Some may leave simply for a few hours. A brief escape into a nearby city, where one can find other gay men and lesbians, fulfills a basic human need to have a space, any space, in which we can be comfortable with who we are. Unfortunately, because of the clandestine nature of Southern homosexuality, those comfortable spaces are seedy bars on a dark back street "the other side of town." I have met people who drive over a hundred miles one way just to sit for a few hours without fear of attack or social retribution. Of course, some leave never to return to their hometown hell.

Those of us who migrated to the city created spaces where we could feel safe and got on with our lives. Over the last 30 years our politics, and our disposable incomes, have began to make headway in securing our rights to jobs, homes, and even families. More large corporations include "sexual orientation" in equal opportunities policies, and offer equal employee benefits to same-sex partners. Our political activism focusses on partnership rights, child custody rights, and health care rights. At the end of the century we can look back at our achievements since the 1969 Stonewall riots and be proud. We can also be pretty damn smug about our rural cousins: "Why the hell don't they just leave?" I for one sit in a whole lot milder moral climate than the hellacious South. But moving is not always the answer. Believe me, I have moved well over 20 times in my 30-odd years. And my self – the voices of my past, my love of the South, the values I acquired as a child and as an adult – always moves with me. As my pa says, you can take the girl out of the country, but you can't take the country out of the girl.

At this juncture perhaps I should tell you a bit more about me and my pa. New folks often ask me how my father, as a Bible Belt preacher, handles the fact that I am a lesbian. My answer is fairly simple, his love for me is consistent with his theology. John Wesley, founder of Methodism, taught a doctrine of social justice. Much of his ministry was with the extreme poor in north London, teaching them to read and write. So the backbone of the Methodist church has been a tradition of social justice. Obviously now, there are those in the church who set boundaries on how far such justice should extend. But not my pa. As an alcoholic who has been sober for over 30 years, the kinds of people he ministered with were not your average church members. Late on Saturday nights he would begin writing his sermon, partly because he procrastinated until the last minute, but mostly because seeing his study light on, troubled folks would know they were welcome to visit. His study, and our living room, were often occupied by people I never saw in church on Sunday morning. Dad was always honest about who he was, about his own struggles and limitations, and about the unconditional love of God. He wasn't in the business of saving people on the street corner. He was there to listen, to help if he could, and to let people know that someone cared.

Nevertheless, it wasn't easy to tell my parents I was a lesbian. Worried about losing parental love, and the reaction of their parish, I attempted to keep it from them for a number of years. But they ain't dumb. When I did finally tell them, they had known all along. While I had been struggling internally, they had been as well. Their reaction was consistent with their values, their theology, and their lives: unconditional love. Over the years we have talked about my life, they have read books for parents of gay and lesbian children, and we have both grappled with the reactions of other family members. When confronted with one who insists homosexuality is a sin, dad respects their right to interpret the scriptures and simply notes that there are lots of "sins" in the Bible for which we do not hate and ostracize people. As a recovering alcoholic, Pa never had much time for "good church people" who thought sinners had no place in God's community.

There are many Christians who liken homosexuality to alcoholism. It is a way in which they can construct it as something to which individuals are predisposed – either genetically or through learned behavior. But as a sin, it is something they need to stop doing. This kind of argument is used by those who will agree that homosexuality is innate or socially constructed but that it should not be acted upon, or that it can be cured. According to a *Newsweek* poll, 56 percent of Americans believe "gay men and lesbians can change their sexual orientation through therapy, will power or religious conviction."[19] Fortunately for me, mom and dad know this is just who I am, the way God made me. They do not believe I am a sinner simply because I am a lesbian. For them, and on this point I agree, sin is much more about how one treats another person. Judgment. Hate. Those are sins.

UNCONDITIONAL LOVE

Given that I am not a regular churchgoer, it seems kind of odd for me to hold on to a notion of "sin." But then again, we all have an inkling about right or wrong behavior. We all have values. Of course we differ about what those values are or should be. Individuals, I reckon, begin to acquire values from childhood and then construct or reconstruct them as we grow up negotiating our encounters in the world. Gay men and lesbians who are children of the rural South, began this process in the middle of Bible Belt Christianity. Whether or not we grew up in the church, the gender norms of Christianity affected our lives. For some who believed in the Christian Right's interpretation, homosexuality was to be hated, even if it meant self hatred. For some who heard only hatred, Christianity, and maybe all spirituality, was to be rejected. For some, spiritual fulfillment was sought outside of organized religion. Still others have chosen not to give up on Christianity, just yet. Instead they chose to build churches based on unconditional love.

Perhaps then it is unsurprising that many Southern gay men and lesbians are flocking to churches based on this accepting love. Membership in the Metropolitan Community Church, and other churches[20] opening their doors to gay men and lesbians, has grown enormously in the last 10 years. Pews are filling up with those tossed aside by mainstream Christianity. Curious as ever, I decided to visit a couple of "gay churches" on my way across the South. As an ex-lay pastor, I was interested in the daily life of the church: how many members did they have? What did that membership look like? What areas of ministry were they active in? So while I was in Houston, I met up with Rev. Mobley, an African-American woman who had grown up in the Southern Baptist church. A vivacious and deeply spiritual woman, she was full of excitement about her parish:

MCC in Houston celebrated its 20th anniversary last spring. In the beginning a handful of people, five or six, decided to meet in their home and put a call out to anyone who wanted to start a church for gays and lesbians and to meet at this address ... they petitioned the MCC in Dallas to help start a church in Houston. Somebody from MCC in Dallas came on weekends to meet with the group here – leading Bible studies and offering the sacrament to people who were denied the sacrament at other churches. So that group grew too big for a living room. They started meeting in a bicycle shop – put the bikes aside and put some chairs out, we had a church. Then the meeting grew too big for that and we rented a little building ... The church right now has a membership of about 370, attendance is well over 400 every week ... It's a very strong church, very stable church, has excellent lay leadership and fairly mature Christians. I'm on [the] staff full-time as an associate. We are getting people all the time and we are adding new members.

We require a membership class as an introduction to spiritual gifts which helps to identify what their strengths and gifts are and how they can serve the church. They look at the areas of opportunity for serving in our church, so that as they become members, they are involved and not just coming on Sundays for church and leaving. One class looks at the history of our church and faith statements and various committees and structures and what we believe in and why we emphasize diversity. We talk about our understanding, our affirmation of sexuality. It's also a chance for us to make sure that we are not missing anything – like why you really want to join. Because if they haven't really made a commitment to Christ, we really need to know that. We talk about what it means to be a Christian first. Joining the church is meaningless if you haven't committed your life to Christ, because that is what the Church is all about.

Our membership is very diverse, men and women, about half and half. African-Americans make up at least 10 percent – it looks like what the country looks like – there are Spanish, maybe another 5 or 6 percent. There are old people and young people. We have women having babies, and there are men who have fathered children from previous marriages who, if the kids live with them, they come and if they are only with them certain weekends or in the summer time they bring them. We do have children's programming in our church. Our music program is wonderful and a children's choir. For the last five years, and probably longer than that, they have had a children's sermon in the midst of their regular worship ... Sometimes there's only two kids, sometimes there's 20–25. Right after the children's sermon, the smallest ones can go to what we call "children's church" and it's kind of a story hour for them. Or they can rehearse for the children's choir. There is an adult class that meets during Sunday school time, and as we get kids in various groups enough to have a class we develop a class for them. We have adult Bible study on Wednesday nights for anyone in the church who wants to come. That's every Wednesday, right after the 30-minute worship service.

There are all kinds of age groups. There are some heterosexuals in our church, a few. Every now and then we get a bi-racial heterosexual couple who just don't hook up to other churches. And so they feel more comfortable here. There's always a mixture of races. There are a lot of biracial men couples, and a few bi-racial women couples so it's no big thing and they just feel more comfortable. Divorced people, and certainly bisexual people, transgender people, are in our church and active and present and visible. So it's really the world. It's a wonderful church, and very diverse.

As it turns out, MCC Houston is a good size congregation with fairly normal church activities. There was a bit of me, however, that wondered if they were just an exception. So when I landed in New Orleans, I sought out the local MCC pastor to find out what they were up to in the one Southern city in which moral decadence is the norm. He began by telling me a bit about the urban moral landscape:

We generally talk about three areas in Louisiana: the area north I would say definitely is part of the Bible Belt; the area south is almost entirely Arcadian/French influenced by the Catholic church; then New Orleans is just like a place all unto itself. It has both of those influences really strong as well as having the urban issues that are prevalent in the other major American cities.

We have more than our share of decadence in the city, but it's not, to use antiquated inaccurate terms, "the Sodom and Gomorra of America." That's simply not the case. There is a very small group of people who do over indulge in a variety of ways whether sexually,

141

ingestion of illegal substances, etc. The priorities of the city are a good time and good food – you ask almost anybody and those will be the top two priorities. And so, if a good time is a priority in your life in this context, there are going to be people who push it to the extreme.

So this city is quite unique. The role of the Roman Catholic church in this social climate is incredible and the Roman Catholic church permeates every level of the political action that takes place in this context. The city is a polarized city in almost every sense of the word, racially, economically. We have this very strong Roman Catholic influence but we also have a very strong Pentecostal church influence that runs through this city. So, it's a city of dichotomy and division. That is probably the biggest challenge that I have had as the pastor. It's also the greatest hope we have. If we can embrace the diversity that we have here, if we can deal with the issues that we come up against because of this systematic oppression – deal with them in a constructive way – then we will be able to become the church that we have been called to be and to do the ministry work, the gospel work here in the city.

The congregation is about 50 members. We have about equal attendance of women and men. We also have a handful of transsexuals who attend our church services. We have probably 20 percent people of color that attend and 80 percent European-Americans.

Each Sunday we have a children's Sunday school during worship time for adults. Children are included in part of the worship service and then they go off and do their Sunday school while we have the sermon. It has really grown – we didn't have any to start with and then we had one, then we had three, then we had 12. We have had up to 15 children in a service at one time. There are some in the congregation that don't understand why we have these "paper rattlers." But I have a place in my heart for the children among us. I feel very deeply that it's a responsibility to ensure that they are raised in an educating, tolerating, accepting, nurturing environment.

One of my roles is as ambassador to the community ... at Mardi Gras we did a public awareness campaign – the church noting that "it's good to enjoy, it's good to celebrate, but remember to be responsible" – and we had little packets made up with worship times and that basic theology statement and there were inserts of condoms. We participate in the Pride Parade, in the AIDS day service.

We're just now starting to do public outings where we, as a group,
go to have fun or participate in an event to publicly identify ourselves as a community church for gay men and lesbians.

Those are the primary ways that we are out there in the community. We also stage things that draw the community into the
church. In old fashion terms, that's called evangelism. The art on
the wall is an opportunity for local artists to express their faith
during a special part of the church season. So each season the art in
the church rotates and we invite the artists and their friends in for a
reception. We did an Easter egg hunt, to support our AIDS ministry, in the public park and invited the whole neighborhood to come
and participate. We did a spaghetti dinner that we really intention-
ally invited every one that we could think of from anywhere that
had anything to do with a member of our congregation to come to
and that was a huge success. We also provide services for the queer
community but are open to the whole community – memorial services, a support group for HIV infected people – the focus of which
is spiritual.

We have made a real specific attempt to be open to the neighborhood. Making sure that they know that we are here and that we are
neighbors. In fact we had neighborhood watch meetings, organized
a watch for crime, etc., here in the sanctuary. The neighbors come
and participate in that way within the church structure. There have
been a number of times when we have had fundraising breakfasts,
or yard sales, and the people from the street always come. So, we
are pretty well accepted.

After hearing about the religious diversity in the city, I asked
about his relationship with ministers of other churches. He
confirmed what is often the case for MCC members – they are
marginalized by their fellow Christians: "There is a city-wide
ministerial association that has made it clear that we are not
welcome to join. There are a couple of other organizations that
would be willing to accept us, but we have chosen to relate to other
communities of faith in an ongoing informal relationship." Up in
Houston, things were a bit better. Rev. Mobley noted, there has
been *some* co-operation amongst churches around the local gay
community:

Three years ago now, a young man who was a banker, was killed, gay bashed. Kids, they caught. They were just out having fun and they wanted to beat up "queers." There are many groups holding marching rallies. And the area clergy got together for a press conference at the spot where this guy was killed and said this was unacceptable. We don't care what people's sexual orientation is, no one deserves to be hunted down like this by some mob, and beaten to death. We are not going to stand for it, this is our neighborhood too. Our trust is in this community and we call for tolerance and acceptance and we will not put up with this. So I was real pleased that at least half and half, straight clergy and gay clergy were making that sort of statement together.

Whenever organizations are doing things in which they invite churches across the board, we are always one of them. Sometimes they are churches that are not in your traditional, liberal mode that have managed to develop a conscience about AIDS and suffering and that people need to be treated with compassion and respect. So we are present whenever there's inter-denominational stuff happening.

But there are a couple of Baptist churches and maybe a Church of Christ that has people in the bar district leafleting and really harassing gay men and lesbians coming in and out of the bars – "Turn away from your sin and be saved." A few people in our church have really worked at putting together a response to that and made some tracts that say "God loves me just as I am." So we're educating them a little bit.

We will hear more about the tactics of "saving gays" a little later, but there was something else I wanted to know about these two: what had their spiritual journey been? In other words, how had they dealt with coming out of the closet and the "call to the ministry"? The pastor in New Orleans shared only briefly about his background and "natural" progression into MCC leadership:

My parents professed to be Roman Catholic and expected us to participate in the church. But there was no participation on the part of the family. The family had no role in the church. The church had no control over how the family operated, etc. I was allowed to go to church, get what I wanted and then come home. I first saw a calling

144

when I was in junior high and was told by my family – who really weren't too happy on the idea of Roman Catholicism – that they didn't think that was a good idea. So I put it on the back burner until I was more independent and adult and got exposed to a situation where I could not only be expressive of my Christian faith, but could also express it fully as a gay man.

I heard about this MCC church and my partner and I thought we had been missing going to church. He had been raised in one tradition, I had in another. But we kind of felt maybe it's time to go back to church and we went and I would say the rest is history. From the first time that I attended I felt welcomed. Although they did things I didn't understand coming from a Roman Catholic background, I stayed and within a year I had been drawn into a leadership position. From there it was just a natural course of events. It isn't an easy transition for a lot of gay men who feel called to be leaders within the Christian church.

Rev. Mobley would agree. The transition wasn't easy for her as a lesbian who had already reached a leadership role in the Baptist church. Her story captures the extent of rejection one can feel when asked to leave the church, and the elation of coming to terms with both one's sexuality and spirituality. In order for her journey to be better understood, I have chosen to include a large section of her story here:

I went to Hardin Simmons University, a Baptist university in Texas, moved to Atlanta to go to seminary, graduated, ... I worked for the next five years as a career home missionary with the Southern Baptist Home Mission group. They asked the inevitable "Are you a lesbian, or what?" and I said "Well, does it matter? What difference does it make? What do you think about my work?" "Well, if you are not a lesbian, then you tell us. If you can't say you're not, then we need your resignation." Oh, in other words lie or get fired.

In Atlanta, I was serving on the staff of the Atlanta Baptist Association basically doing work with students who needed field work experience in Baptist Mission Centers. It was very interesting. I loved the work. It was fun. I worshipped there on Sundays. But I was also involved with the Metropolitan Community Church there. A seminary friend got me involved as a friend of the church ... I eventually joined when I was asked to leave my job.

If you have been to seminary, MCC require a year's experience under another Pastor. They also require everyone to take a sexuality course which most people don't get in seminary no matter what school you go to ... You could then take other courses: church history, Protestant Bible, preaching. It is very good – you get preparation for working in the local church. I then was interviewed by a team – now called the Board of Ordained Ministers – to ascertain the level of commitment for full time ministry and also understanding of where you are theologically.

I certainly was not aware of my sexuality when I was really small but I was already doing cute little, like baby dyke things, like falling in love with my baby-sitter and telling my mom I was going to marry a woman when I got big, that sort of stuff. "Oh you're cute," Mom used to say when I was in first grade, by the time I was in third grade I told Mom not to say that any more. I'm not cute, but I am still going to marry a girl. So I got the message, I toned it down, chilled out, tried to, you know, conform, but it was clearly not working. I remember real clearly when my mom said I couldn't wear pants and had to wear dresses, I couldn't climb any more trees, just stop it, you know. So it was like "Oh, people are running my life here, what's going on?" By the time I was about ten or twelve, I certainly knew that I was very attracted to girls, that I didn't really like boys, and wasn't going to go through a "boy crazy" phase. But I needed to at least pretend to like them enough to not get beat up. So I just went into neutral, but it was easy because I was in a religious family and my grandfather was Baptist preacher and my whole family was in church. I became a Christian when I was ten years old, that was fairly real for me in terms of receiving Christ into my life and knowing that I wanted to belong to God. I did belong to God, I wanted to be in the family of Christ. So to think that maybe liking girls didn't please God did worry me for a while but then ... it's like "Well, God knows I've been like this ever since I was in the world." Where did these feelings come from? I'm not generating them. They're just there and it's like a given. So I had to think about what to do with these feelings. So I decided fairly early on that maybe it was best not to act on it. That it was OK to feel that and I was fine. God knew I felt this way and God could take it away any time God wanted to. So by the time I got into high school, it was really more serious, because I was falling in love – a little more hormonal activity. I was wanting to do things with girls that clearly wasn't cool. So I decided that I wasn't going to be sexually active at all. I was a virgin through college – no boys, no girls, going out with the appropriate gender when it was called for ... when you have to have a date or an escort. But I was clearly not interested in anybody.

By the time I finished college I decided it was time – sex is not going away. People have to deal with it their whole lives, and now is the time for me to focus on it. So that was the first time that I became active, sexually involved with anyone, a woman first. Then I told Mom that I was a lesbian and she felt like it would certainly be worth my time to get on the pill and explore sex. I thought, "Now all my life I have been told not to do this, now all of a sudden it's OK." I thought "What do I know, maybe she's right." So I got on the pill for about three or four months and calculated exactly when I would have sex with this one guy. I thought "Well, if it works, maybe it will be fine. If it doesn't, nothing gained, nothing lost." So, did that, it was a hoax. I thought women wait their whole lives for this! Never again. I thought God must be laughing. This is a joke. I'm through with it, so much for that. I never did it again. I never felt the need to. I didn't like it the first time, why try to make yourself like something you're not going to like? I already know what I like, so let's go with that program. So from that time on, I have just followed my own inner drive about who I was attracted to.

When I was about 16, I read through the whole book of Romans. That passage in the first chapter which is supposed to be so clearly anti-gay convinced me that it was unnatural for me to try and make myself go against my nature.[21] That passage is not talking about some natural order that men have to be with women, and women with men, but rather people have given up what's natural for them. So for me that passage began to make it clear that if I was going to be anything less than authentic, that is what displeases God. Dishonesty. For me to pretend to be something I am not to appease society would be making God angry. So authenticity was more important and to do what was natural and normal for me. The big point of the Book of Romans is that it's not your sexuality – it's all about your faith in Christ. So gay people, straight people, bisexual people all have to be saved the same way, by trusting Christ and not their own ability to keep the law or live by any particular set of rules. It's all about a relationship with God. I knew that my relationship with God was intact and I was grateful for that and so it gave me a great sense of peace. That God knew who I was. He made me this way, accepts me for who I am and wanted me to use my whole life, including my sexuality, to bring glory to God.

Rev. Mobley's story was about coming to terms with both her call to ministry and her "God-given" sexuality. A young man in Dallas, once a leader in a large charismatic congregation tells a similar story of rejection, and of finding a home:

My name is Darrell. I am 31 years old. I currently hold three degrees – an undergraduate in theology, an undergraduate in business and an associate in marketing. I am currently working on my MBA for business administration.

My parents raised us Church of Christ. When my parents divorced, the church took offense to my mother divorcing. So we basically didn't go to church for a little bit. I was the first in my family to want to go back, but I was very angry with the Church of Christ for how they had treated my mother. So I went to a charismatic church now known as Church on the Rock. Just to name a few things that I did at the Church on the Rock at various times: I was over the single men's ministry; I was over the children's ministry; I did a vacation Bible school which had 300 kids. Then I moved to what they call care groups, which are small groups where people communicate on a more intimate level. So I was over that and I was a single young man.

Well I moved and I was commuting to the headquarters working as an administrator. I would set up people for speakers, get people to come in – when acts or groups would come in I would take care of them, the hotel, the car, the food, and the schedules. After I moved, I went to the church located closer to me and I was told that because I was a single man I couldn't do anything in the church. I said "Why can't I do this? I have done this before, at the larger church, and now you are telling me I can't do this." They said that if I was married, then it would work. That really hurt me a lot. I couldn't be anything in leadership because I wasn't married. So I decided to stay home one day from church and I felt such a relief. I was so committed to this church that I was there any time they asked me to be there. It was a whole month before they even called to find out where I was, what had happened, what was going on. That really hurt me, a lot.

We [Darrell and his partner] felt, separately as well as together, that our spiritual needs were not being met and we needed that spiritual part of us. But I didn't feel that it was right to be gay and a Christian at the same time and I was scared to death of the MCC. A friend of ours had asked us go to Church with him and so we went to MCC. It wasn't the horror story that I thought it was. After going a while I really felt that this was the church for me. I really enjoyed it because it was like a new beginning. I really believe there is an emotional, physical and spiritual side of a person. I actually believe that you are not truly whole until you have a balance of these. I have been there over a year now, they have asked me to be over the single men's ministry. The largest gay/lesbian church in the world! For me that is a really big honor.

Darrell's story does not end there. As an active member of the charismatic church he had been involved in a ministry devoted to "saving gays." A vast array of denominations have entered into the ministry of changing someone from homosexual to heterosexual. The impact of this message to those brought up in the church cannot be understated. Testimonials of ex-homosexuals litter Christian magazines. I have included a couple here which exemplify the hidden need in many Southern gay men and lesbians who continue to search for Christian acceptance.[22] David, a native of Georgia, left his rural town and headed for San Francisco in the late 1970s. He "joined the gay bar scene" but he continues, "that didn't fill the void in my heart, and I turned to drugs and alcohol." He eventually returned to the South and got involved in a local church where the pastor "helped me see that my homosexuality was learned behavior, and that I could choose to leave it ... I know now that the emotional make-up of homosexual behavior is rooted in self-hatred, and an overwhelming sense of being different from heterosexual men, and therefore, not being able to relate to them." As a married man with five children, he notes that they "remind me of joy I would have missed if I had continued believing the lie that homosexual men cannot change." Similarly, Jami, from rural Texas tells that her college roommate led her to lesbianism. She had a few monogamous relationships with women but points out that it was difficult to get out of "lesbian society" because of financial hardship: "Perhaps you've read that homosexuals have a lot of money – which may be true in the male gay community – but in the lesbian society, you usually have two $5 or $6 wage-earners living together." She continues her story noting her involvement with the MCC:

> In the 12 years I was a lesbian, I never went to a gay-pride meeting, never paraded down mainstreet, and never knew a pedophile. I still wanted a relationship with God, so I attended a Metropolitan Community Church, where gay people are welcomed with open arms. We used Bibles with translations that eliminated the word "homosexual." That's how much we were deluding ourselves.

While she eventually married a male childhood friend, it was the words of a lesbian ex-partner that worried her most: "She would always ask me, 'Do you really think if the Lord came back, we would go to heaven?' The question haunted me, I'd wake up in the middle of the night, thinking, what if the Lord came back? That was my greatest fear, being left behind." Her "greatest fear," learned undoubtedly at an early age, was to be left out of the Lord's flock. Instead of sharing a message of God's love, organized Christianity played on her fear. In almost every urban gay village in the South you will find an extensive ministry to "save gays." At one time Darrell, himself, had been doing just that on the streets of the Dallas gay village.

"Bringing gays to Christ," i.e. saving them from the sin of homosexuality, is a tactic of confronting gay men and lesbians as they walk down the street. Of course, those of us who are approached can simply ignore them and walk away. Indeed when my partner and I went out in Dallas recently, that is exactly what we did. The look on her British face when she realized what they were saying was one of overwhelming astonishment: how completely bizarre to be accosted in the street and told she was going to hell! As I said in the introduction, we all come from strange cultures, but I realized then just how strange mine was to her. If you have lived there, grown up surrounded by Southern Christianity, being approached on the street and asked about the cleanliness of your soul seems fairly normal. And anyone even hinting at its uncleanliness, leads to great self-reflection. That's what this "ministry" is counting on: guilt and self-hatred. Darrell tells how it's done:

When I was getting my theological degree, I got involved with the street ministry and one of them was called Gay Prostitution Ministry. We/they would go out on the streets of the gay village. They come out on Fridays or Saturdays, they pass out tracts. They've always got someone in the group that was a gay man or lesbian and they are saved and brought to God. I used to be that kind of person out there preaching on the streets, on going to hell for being gay. And it's funny how 10 years later, almost the same street, I go on dates.

When you go for your degree you have to put 20 hours into one of the ministries. One of them is the Gay Prostitution Ministry in which you spend one night a week with the group praying – if you didn't make the prayer time, you couldn't go out that week – then that Friday you would meet to go out. They would pray beforehand, everybody would gets tracts, every male with a female partner, if there's an odd number then either, depending on the person they would probably stick with the leader, or they would go like two guys and a girl. They had rules and regulations never to go into any of the gay establishments for whatever reason. If you had to go to the bathroom there is a designated area. You'd either hold hands with your partner or you'd go arm in arm with your partner, or you'd stick very close to your partner. You were never to leave your partner. The leader would often have people who would be "watchers" – all they do is watch the group to make sure they do not get harassed so that no one hits them or anything. If there is any problem, they step in.

So you say something like, "Do you know Jesus loves you?" –
you always ask an open ended question. Sometimes they would do it
with a baiting question to make you answer. If they can just get you
to take a tract that's half the battle. The great thing is to just get
you to start talking. That's half the battle because if you take that
tract and you put it in your pocket, and after you have been to the
bar, you go home, you get up the next day and you pull everything
out of your pocket and you see that tract and you start reading it.
It's got some stuff on it and their name and number. If they get you
to talking ... "You're not happy here, why are you doing this?"
Then if that evening you decide that this isn't what I want to do any
more – "I don't want to be gay, or I don't want to like this lifestyle
any more" – they would pray with you. They would give you a
phone number, get your number. They would counsel you. They
would want to do a follow up with you later, like meet with you
somewhere neutral – not in the gay part of town. There would be
like three people, two guys and a girl, or two girls and a guy. They'd
want to recommend a church to you. They'd recommend that if you
were doing drugs or drinking you should stop. If you were living
with gay people, you should move out. If you were working at a gay
establishment you should look for another job. If MCC ever came
up they would say that was not the place to go. Basically, sever
yourself from the gay community. Then they would send you to a
church and they would do maybe one more follow up at the church.
In the year that I worked with them I think there was 16 people
[who were brought in this way], mostly men. But I don't know,
because once they get you in a church you're done.

Now, I'm not there to debate them, because I know the Bible as
well as they do, maybe even better. But I don't feel you can win
someone over by debate. I really believe that one of the many ways
you can win someone over is by your testimony, by your life, by
what comes out of you. They already have an image of me just
because I am down there. They already have their mind set, you
know. I am not there to convert them over to be gay but they are
there to convert me. I feel that's something that God has created in
me and if they can't understand that ... But then there's people like
myself and others who go to the MCC who, I feel lead a very whole
life – I meet my spiritual man, I meet my physical man and my emotional man. I would like to see myself married with children, just

like my mother and father, just like other couples. I know people that are gay and they're living a straight lifestyle. They married a woman, they have children. I respect them, I am not putting them down for that because they have chosen to live that lifestyle. I believe don't try to be something you are not.

Leaving the charismatic church, coming out, and now an active member in an MCC church, Darrell's journey certainly hasn't been easy. As he speaks of those in the Gay Prostitution Ministry, I can't help believing that he continues to grieve that his former church will never understand the damage they caused. The rejection by his church was not the only worry on Darrell's mind:

> Right now my family is having a very difficult time with my lifestyle because, I mean they freaked out that I go to the clubs. They freaked out that I just went to the parade ... They want me to be straight again. I said, "You want me to live a lie, that's what you want me to do. You want me to be with someone I don't want to be with, to make you happy." What's important is for me to be happy and for me to be what I am ... But you know I have had to sit down and think: I have to be prepared to lose my family which has meant everything to me.

The loss of spiritual support, of place in God's community, and the potential loss of family are overwhelming for Southern gay men and lesbians. Driving through the backroads of my homeland, passing through one small town after the next, I wondered how many gay men and lesbians grew up in each of the hundreds of little churches I saw. Each time I stopped and visited with folk, I attempted to find out what they believed about homosexuality. One old man simply looked me straight in the eye, shook his head, and walked away. Another woman, doing her Saturday shopping, took a deep breath and said, "Now, we don't talk about such things around here." Most of the local pastors either escorted me briskly out the door or took the opportunity to inquire about the status of my soul. A couple mentioned the local "homo-sex-u-al" adding that they had heard he "mo-lested" young boys. I realize my methodology was rather random on this point, but surely gay men and lesbians who left their rural homes for Southern cities came from somewhere. With this thought in my mind, I glanced in the rear-view mirror only to see the blue eyes I share with my family. What would they say to a stranger?

As a part-time youth minister during college, I traveled every Sunday out to a little bitty church in the boondocks. I would spend the afternoon and early evening visiting with the church teens, giving a devotional and playing volleyball. One evening just as I was leaving a young woman walked up to the car and asked to talk. We sat down on the swings in the parking lot and she began to tell me about her first term away at college. After 20 minutes of beating around the bush, she got to her problem. She had fallen in love. "Why," I inquired, "is this a problem?" Tears began to roll down her cheeks as she whispered, "with a woman." Now I had known this young woman for a couple of years. I knew how the other kids, the other church kids, treated her. She was a reader, a loner, a tomboy that hadn't learned quite how to be a lady. I watched her struggle through high school and eventually to make it out of this dusty town with high hopes for the future. I knew her parents. I also knew our conservative pastor. Sitting in the winter sun, watching her tears flow, and knowing her complete vulnerability, I knew my reaction was crucial. She had sought me out – someone not much older than her, but in a position to offer her guidance. Glancing at the pristine white steeple atop the sanctuary, I thought about my secret lesbian partner at home waiting for me.

At the close of this chapter, it is that moment which haunts me. For it is the complexity of that moment which captures the stories, and beliefs, above. The storm raging in America, and reaching fever pitch in the Bible Belt, between homosexuality and Christianity is not about the battle between good and evil. If it were easy to clarify those, to choose consistently between those, there would be no need for spirituality, or divine forgiveness. Homosexuality and Christianity can, and do, live together. And it does not have to entail anyone's sacrifice of beliefs, or of self. But, when Christianity demonizes homosexuals – names homosexuals as Satan – when it lays the foundation for social marginalization – enacting "anti-gay" legislation – when it incites people to crime, to family rejection, to hate, it is, quite simply, failing to live its own message of God's love. An unconditional love that *knows* life's complexities.

NOTES

1 W. J. Blumenfeld and D. Raymond (eds), *Looking at Gay and Lesbian Life* (Boston, MA: Beason Press, 1993), p. 245.

2 Baptist minister quoted in L. Scanzoni and V. R. Mollenkott, *Is the Homosexual My Neighbor?* (San Francisco, CA: Harpers & Row, 1980), p. 2.

3 J. Leland and M. Miller, "Can Gays Convert?" *Newsweek*, August 17, 1998.

4 *Ibid.*, p. 50.

5 *USA Today*, May 8, 1996.

6 Photo in M. Segrest and L. Zeskind, *Quarantines and Death* (Atlanta, GA: Center for Democratic Renewal, 1989), p. 16.

7 "Families shocked by homosexual celebration at Magic Kingdom," *AFA Journal*, August 1996, p. 8.

8 "Pro-Family Activists Make Their Voices Heard," *AFA Journal*, November/December 1996, p. 16.

9 AFA Statement of Purpose listed in each journal.

10 *AFA Journal*, April 1996, pp. 33–9.

11 *Ibid.*, pp. 37–9.

12 *Ibid.*

13 For further reading see, for example, M. Kaplan, *Sexual Justice* (London: Routledge, 1997); V. Samar, *The Right to Privacy* (Philadelphia PA: Temple University Press, 1991).

14 In addition, on average women earn less than men and therefore lesbians would earn less than heterosexual men.

15 J. Sears, *Growing Up Gay in The South: Race, Gender and Journeys of the Spirit* (Binghamton, NY: Harrington Park Press, 1991).

16 *Ibid.*, pp. 37–9.

17 P. Chesler, "Sister, fear has no place here," *On the Issues*, Fall 1994, p. 27.

18 A more detailed account of my argument concerning rural lesbians can be found in "Getting Your Kicks on Route 66: Stories of gay and lesbian life in rural America *c*. 1950–1970s," in R. Phillips *et al.* (eds), *Non-Metropolitan Sexualities* (London: Routledge, 1999).

19 Poll result reported in J. Leland and M. Miller, "Can Gays Convert?" *Newsweek*, August 17 1998, p. 48.

20 For example, see *Open Hands: Resources for Ministries Affirming the Diversity of Human Sexuality* (Chicago, IL: Open Hands), a quarterly magazine listing Presbyterian, Methodist, Congregational, First Christian, and Lutheran churches welcoming gay men and lesbians.

21 "God gave them up to dishonorable passions. Their women exchanged natural relations for unnatural, and the men likewise gave up natural relations with women and were consumed with passion for one another, men committing shameless acts with men and receiving in their own persons the due penalty for their error." (Romans 1:26–27.)

22 D. Davis, "Filling My Hearts Need" and J. Breedlove, "The Transforming Power of God" in *Good News*, January/February 1996, pp. 22–4.

Chapter Six

WHAT THE HELL DID YOU DO THAT FOR?

As noted in Chapter 1, *Below the Belt* is my story book. In visiting with Southern folks, in retelling their stories, I have endeavored to discover how I ended up *here*. My route was a rather complex journey. I took the winding backroads, not the Interstate highways, leading the reader directly to where I currently find myself. When I was a kid and my ma caught me telling a lie, she would ask me if I was "telling a story." And I have no doubt that some, probably on the Christian Right, will think I am fibbin' here. Hand on heart, I have tried to (re)tell these stories, including my own, as honestly as possible. I went fishing, but I didn't catch a whopper. Much to the dismay of the Christian Right I didn't prove that laws need to reflect their version of morality. Likewise, no doubt to the dismay of some feminists or gay and lesbian activists, I didn't prove that Christianity is "the enemy." My intention was simply to paint a picture of Southern culture, one that I think captures the complexity of gender in the Bible Belt. In reflecting upon my own journey I have in turn held up a mirror to my Southern homeland. While I have tried to do so honestly, I have not done so objectively. Such thirty-something ponderings may appear confessional, perhaps even apologetic. Certainly in writing this piece I have faced my own complex feelings about growing up in the South, about moving beyond Bible Belt Christianity, about (re)locating my self in a cultural and moral home.

Reflection can be a learning experience. But only if it moves one beyond navel gazing. In his travel book, Bill Bryson offers a picture of American rural culture from the comfort of his car. Similarly, academics have a habit of offering "scientific" accounts, or sociopolitical theories, of cultural nuances, in which they have little personal investment. Given that I am writing about my home, about my communal pool of values, I obviously have an interest in

157

fostering appreciation of those values as well as in shaping their future. Exploring the Bible Belt has assisted my understanding how I ended up *here*. But it has not led me to a dead-end.

The last half of this century has witnessed intense social change. Feminism, the civil rights movement, the gay and lesbian movement, economic globalization, and the technological revolution have challenged collective values, as well as the way in which policies reflect those values. For example, we profess a belief in equality. But before the civil rights movement such equality did not extend to Southern Black people. We believe American democracy rests upon the idea of freedom. But until women challenged the policies which kept them out of employment or on low pay, they had no hope of freedom. However, some argue that the social change stemming from the 1960s was the beginning of the end of social stability based on communal values, and that the result of this intense social change has left us completely unable to delineate any shared values. For example, conservatives argue that the persistent challenge to what we once claimed as valuable, e.g. "the family," has led to the complete breakdown of worthy social institutions, e.g. "the family." In fact, critics of this postmodern era defined it as nothing less than an endorsement of value relativism.[1]

I remember when I was about four, my eldest brother joined the army. On the night that he left I was inconsolable. When mom and dad finally calmed me down, I told them that he was going to "end up in a hole." You see, like most teenage boys, my brother could be a real pain. He had a habit of "backtalkin'" which would always get him into trouble. I was convinced that he would "backtalk" a sergeant who would then punish him by putting him "in a hole." I knew about "the hole" – I had seen it on TV. It took them a few minutes to put together the picture in my head with the news footage of Vietnam POWs kept in holes in the ground. Eventually mom and dad assured me that while my brother was testing out his manhood around the house, once he got into the army he would show (other) adults respect. He would be a good boy. As a child they lessened the complexity of war with a satisfactory explanation of my brother's ability to respect authority. That is what adults do –

protect children from the complexities of life. And while some, the Christian Right for example, may want the state to paternalistically protect them from the complexities of the world, I am not convinced that the majority understand that to be the role of the state.

In addition, acknowledging complexity does not necessarily indicate valuelessness. I would argue that at least one sign of maturity is the ability to acknowledge, to understand, the complexity of life and to struggle to negotiate different needs. Adults, moms in particular, do that everyday. Perhaps then the proliferation of values at the end of this century is a call to negotiate complexity. Jeffery Weeks aptly summarizes the current moral climate:

> We are besieged by value debates. The last decade or so has seen a torrent of value-laden arguments, largely from the political and moral right, but also from popes and preachers, ayatollahs, religious revivalists and fundamentalists of various political hues, which tell us unrelentingly how we should live, and whose protagonists do their best to ensure that we conform to their strictures. Yet the overwhelming feeling in our culture is of moral confusion rather than moral certainty ... we actually live with a confusing plurality of values, some particularist, some claiming a universal validity, but each rooted in different traditions, histories and theoretical and political trajectories, and many of them in stark contradiction, one to the other.[2]

He advises that "we need to learn how to negotiate the hazards of social complexity and moral diversity."[3] Taking the debate a step further, Martin Hewitt shines a light upon such negotiations, pointing out the challenge of postmodernity and its potentiality. "The challenge of postmodern theory lies in exposing the metanarratives of social, political and moral theory and in recasting their agendas towards diversity and difference, so that the structure of universal and particular interests can be reconstituted."[4] In acknowledging complexity, we may recast social institutions. We are not throwing the valuable baby out with the bathwater. So the abrupt categories in the first lines of this book which "identify" me, do not tell my story. The interesting bit is their overlap, their complexity. How, you may have thought, are all these identities encapsulated in one? Similarly, in the telling of my story, in the retelling of others' stories, I have redressed the stereotypes of the South. The resulting reconstituted, more complex, story is one that is inclusive of voices who had been silenced previously.

The cacophony of voices should not leave us overwhelmed but should challenge us to listen to different sounds, different stories. In her important intervention into contemporary political positioning, *Getting Specific*, Shane Phelan highlights the significance of listening to the specific needs of diverse groups, and individuals:

> If democratic politics is about masses, about numbers and majorities, then all of us who share some fragmented parts of a common dream need to develop the ability to talk to each other. This cannot be done by ignoring differences; it must come by moving through and with them. Our politics, disappointingly enough, must consist of continued patient and impatient struggle with ourselves and those "within" and "without" our "communities" ... We have to stand where we are, acknowledging the contradictions and forging the links between ourselves and other marginal citizens of the world, resisting the temptation to cloak crucial differences with the cloak of universality while also refusing to harden those differences into identities that cannot be crossed. The promise of getting specific is the promise of theorizing, which is to say discussing and working on, the possibility of such a politics.[5]

The assumption of universality, of cultural sameness, of Southern gender/sexual clarity is one which silences voices of difference. Each chapter has attempted to acknowledge the range of voices in the Bible Belt, and to hear their specific relationship to cultural gender/sexual norms. In the voices of "others," we hear the way in which they make sense of the impact of these norms. Every child of the South has, consciously or unconsciously, constructed their identity in relation to rather strict gender/sexual rules. Whether we perceive the air as clear or as stifling, we all live in the atmosphere of the genteel South.

The boys and men of Chapter 2 positioned themselves in relation to the expectations of Southern manhood. And each one, in turn, felt the need to explain how they did, or why they did not, measure up to such expectations. Referring to American men more generally, but I think it is particularly valid for Southern men, Erving Goffman suggests the significance of individual men's relationship to a masculine ideal:

> In an important sense there is only one complete unblushing male in America: a young, married, white, urban, northern, heterosexual Protestant father of college education, fully employed of good complexion, weight, and height, and a recent record in sports. Every American male tends to look out upon the world from this perspective, thus constituting one sense in which one can speak of [a] common value system in America. Any male who fails to qualify in any one of these ways is likely to view himself – during moments at least – as unworthy, incomplete, and inferior.[6]

In the South the specifics may be slightly different, but the point is still relevant: that men struggle to be what society or, they are told, God expects them to be. Hearing their stories we come to understand their positioning. We can know why Bubba is angry, even if we despise the way in which he lashes out. Make no mistake, most here are the beneficiaries of white patriarchy – from the social, political, and economic power given to them as white men. And the gender/moral rules of the Bible Belt certainly place them in a position of power over everyone else.

In addition Southern women attempt to be all that God, or right-wing preachers, want them to be. However, in the voices found in Chapter 3, there was an identifiable edge of pain. The middle-class good Christian women who juggle expectations of Biblical proportions could, quite frankly, benefit from Betty Friedan's original call to arms:

> Gradually, without seeing it clearly for quite a while, I came to realize that something is very wrong with the way American women are trying to live their lives today. I sensed it first as a question mark in my own life, as a wife and mother of three small children, half-

guiltily, and therefore half-heartedly, almost in spite of myself using my abilities and education in work that took me away from home ... There was a strange discrepancy between the reality of our lives as women and the image to which we were trying to conform, the image that I came to call the feminine mystique.[7]

The discrepancy between the reality of their lives – as working women, as active citizens – and the image they are told to be – submissive, carers – is a sound testament to the ability of men to legitimate their own power. But the power to marginalize, to enforce conformity, does not reside exclusively in male hands. Women, perhaps unconsciously, conspire with male-defined gender norms to ensure that all women conform. Those who do not, Teri, Louise, J.T., have been forced into the prescribed attire of their gender, or have been isolated for their insubordination. Southern clarity may offer easy answers in today's complex world, but it certainly does not make for easy lives.

The complexities haunting chapters 4 and 5 mark the urgency to move beyond "good" v. "evil" political positioning. Abortion, legally permitted by the state, or illegally sought by individual women, is not a public battle between "the seed of the serpent" and "the seed of the woman." It is always, in every case, a personal battle:

> There seems to be two images of women who have an abortion: cold-hearted bitches who have the operation as easily as having a tooth out, regarding it as just another form of contraception, or victims racked by depression, guilt and regret. The truth lies somewhere in between. It's not an easy decision to make. It's somewhat more complex than having a tooth out. Yet you do get over it.[8]

The complexity of such a decision demands respect. A woman does not need to be yelled at as she walks through the doors of a clinic. Yelling does not save lives, it destroys souls. Likewise, the pain of women who have abortions does not need to be forgotten by the pro-choice supporters. Similarly, the complex relationship between Christianity and homosexuality urges us to see the common spiritual ground occupied by many in the Bible Belt. Constructing the closet door as the Gates of Hades, perpetuates a culture of hate – one which sanctions killing, assaulting, harassing, socially marginalizing other human beings. The role of the state, particularly in American democracy founded upon religious freedom and the separation of church and state, should not extend into the private decisions of adults, consenting adults, negotiating their sexual identity.[9]

What then are the lessons of sexuality we can learn from the stories here? Most significantly, cultural gender/sexual norms – polarized masculine/feminine behavior reinforced through social and political regulation – do not serve men or women adequately. They do not map easily onto any one individual's identity. According to the men's and women's stories told here, gender norms serve only to highlight an individual's inadequacy in measuring up to cultural standards. Moreover, in drawing attention to those "inadequacies" they serve as justification for social marginalization. In other words, many of the women and men here are uncomfortable with, or exhausted from, the struggle to live up to Bible Belt gender norms. Those who do publicly act out appropriate gender behavior reap the social rewards, e.g. inclusion. But those who do not – those whose own interests or identity or life circumstances are more complex – are socially excluded.

Now some may note that I am, as they say in England, "teaching my Grandmother to suck eggs" – stating the obvious. Feminists have long challenged the restrictiveness of gender norms. But, as we have noticed, feminism wasn't warmly welcomed by the Bible Belt masses. In addition, it could be argued that young women, while beneficiaries of second-wave feminism, are not falling over themselves to rally the feminist(s) cause. Many "feminist leaders" have found legitimization by casting their politics in inaccessible academic language. This collusion is not surprising, as Joyce Trebilcot notes: "A concept of a philosopher – white, male, oldish, 'wise' – was transmitted to me as a part of the culture in which I was conditioned."[10] Not surprising, perhaps even academically necessary, but it is lamentable nevertheless. The language of theory enables debate, but it sometimes fails to communicate to every intelligent interested reader. And the importance of challenging gender/sexual norms remains a lesson larger society has yet to learn.

In the closing lines of *The History of Sexuality, Vol. 1*, Michel Foucault wonders what people in the future will make of the 20th century's fascination with sexuality:

> They will not be able to understand how a civilization so intent on developing enormous instruments of production and destruction found the time and the infinite patience to inquire so anxiously concerning the actual state of sex; people will smile perhaps when they recall that here were men – meaning ourselves – who believed that therein resided a truth every bit as precious as the one they had already demanded from the earth, the stars, and the pure forms of their thought; people will be surprised at the eagerness with which we went about pretending to rouse from its slumber a sexuality which everything – our discourses, our customs, our institutions, our regulations, our knowledges – was busy producing in the light of day and broadcasting to noisy accompaniment.[11]

Writing this passage in the late 1970s, Foucault could not have known quite the level of sexual commotion that would draw this century to a close. As I have little desire to add to the socio-political clatter on this particular topic, a book about Southern sexuality would not be complete without at least mentioning Arkansas' Ol' Slick Willie.

Briefly, what are some of the lessons of sexuality offered by America's recent public fascination with the President's sex life? At least one lesson is that Clinton did exactly what was expected of him: as a man married to a woman who fails to be submissive, he "naturally" went looking for one who would; as a politician, he "naturally" lied about it. Bubba, or any other "real" Southern man, would have done the same. "So what?" said the voting public. Likewise, Hillary played her role as the good Southern wife: standing by her man. In addition, Monica has reminded us of the expectations we place on young women: success often depends on submitting to the needs of the right man. Similarly, the backlash against the Starr Report proved that America has learned that public morality often hides private immorality, e.g. Jim and Tammy Bakker, Jimmy Swaggart. But in their microscopic search for the sexual "Truth," did the Starr Gang really fail to hear the "noisy" production of these sexual lessons all around us? And if some miss these fairly obvious cultural lessons of sexuality, I doubt the more subtle are getting much attention. For example, after 40 years of feminism, men in general, Clinton in particular, are able to get whatever (whoever?) they/he want by (mis)using power; and that such behavior remains socially, and politically acceptable. Moreover, that it is the *victimization* of Monica – first by Clinton, and then by the press who imprisoned her in the Watergate Hotel and then "dissed" her for eating too many delivered Pizzas – that gave her cultural acclaim. And there is Hillary. Demonized originally because she had a brain, and knew how to use it to get what she wanted, then forced to win public approval by tarting herself up, pretending to bake cookies, and finally swearing allegiance to her untrustworthy husband. Of course, Hillary may have lessons she has yet to teach.

As I boarded the plane back to England, I began to reflect upon my research, and personal, journey through the South. One cannot fully grasp American politics without understanding the extent to which normative Christianity dictates the political, social, and sexual agenda. The comfortable well-established home of that conservative Christianity is the American South. Confederate patriarchy, and white capitalism provide friendship and a neighborly helping hand. And in this genteel atmosphere, gender/sexual clarity perpetuates the ease with which they yield power over all they survey. Gender/sexual complexities are unwelcome here. And anyone caught giving them a home, will be punished, *Below the Belt.*

NOTES

1 For a broad discussion of postmodernism see T. Docherty (ed.), *Postmodernism: A Reader* (Hemel Hempstead: Harvester Wheatsheaf, 1993); C. Jencks (ed.), *The Post-Modern Reader* (London: Academy,

1993); S. K. White, *Political Theory and Postmodernism* (Cambridge: Cambridge University Press, 1991).

2 J. Weeks, "Rediscovering Values," in J. Squires (ed.), *Principled Positions: Postmodernism and the Rediscovery of Value* (London: Lawrence and Wishart, 1993), p. 189.

3 *Ibid.*

4 M. Hewitt, "Social Policy and the question of postmodernism," *Social Policy Review* 6, 1994, p. 48.

5 S. Phelan, *Getting Specific* (Minneapolis, MN: University of Minnesota Press, 1994), pp. 158–9.

6 E. Goffman, *Stigma* (New York: Doubleday, 1968), p. 128.

7 B. Friedan, *The Feminine Mystique* (Harmondsworth: Penguin, 1965).

8 Anne Marie in *Girl Frenzy* No. 6, found in G. Greer, *The Whole Woman* (London: Doubleday, 1999), p. 92. Thanks to Kath Dimmelow for pointing out this resonate quotation.

9 For further reading on the legal and political issues involved, see D. Herman, *Rights of Passage* (Toronto: University of Toronto Press, 1994); M. Kaplan, *Sexual Justice* (London: Routledge, 1997); V. Samar, *The Right to Privacy* (Philadephia: Temple University Press, 1991).

10 J. Trebilcot, *Dyke Ideas: Process, Politics, Daily Life* (New York: SUNY Press, 1994), p. 67.

11 M. Foucault, *The History of Sexuality Vol. 1* (Harmondsworth: Penguin, 1978), pp. 157–8.

BIBLIOGRAPHY

Below the Belt is positioned within a broad context of the books and articles listed here. Many of these have been suggested as further reading about points encountered within the text.

AFA Journal "Families shocked by homosexual celebration at Magic Kingdom" (Tupelo, MS: American Family Association, August 1996).

AFA Journal "Pro-family activists make their voices heard" (Tupelo, MS: American Family Association, November/December 1996).

AFA Journal (Tupelo, MS: American Family Association, April 1996).

Attfield, R., *The Ethics of Environmental Concern* (Oxford: Blackwell, 1983).

Benham, F., "The Way of the Cross: no cheap solutions" (Dallas, TX: Operation Rescue, n.d.).

Blumenfeld, W. J. and Raymond, D. (eds), *Looking at Gay and Lesbian Life* (Boston, MA: Beason Press, 1993).

Bookchin, M., *The Ecology of Freedom* (Palo Alto: Cheshire Books, 1982).

Breedlove, J., "The transforming power of God," in *Good News* (Wilmore, KY, January/February 1996).

Bristow, J., *Sexuality* (London: Routledge, 1997).

Brod, H. (ed.), *The Making of Masculinities* (Boston: Unwin, Hyman, 1987).

Bruce, S., *The Rise and Fall of the New Christian Right: Conservative Protestant Politics in America 1978–1988* (Oxford: Clarendon Press, 1990).

Bryson, B., *The Lost Continent: Travels in Small Town America* (London: Abacus, 1990).

Chesler, P., "Sister, fear has no place here," *On the Issues*, Fall 1994.

Chesler, P., *Women and Madness* (New York: Avon Books, 1972).

Chodorow, N., *The Reproduction of Mothering: Psychoanalysis and the Sociology of Gender* (Berkeley, CA: University of California Press, 1978).

Bibliography

Connell, R. W., *Gender and Power* (Stanford, CA: Stanford University Press, 1987).

Connell, R. W., *Masculinities* (Cambridge: Polity, 1995).

Coole, D., *Women In Political Theory: From Ancient Misogyny to Contemporary Feminism* 2nd edn (London: Harvester Wheatsheaf, 1993).

Daniels, N. (ed.), *Reading Rawls* (Oxford: Blackwell, 1985).

Davis, D., "Filling my heart's need," in *Good News* (Wilmore, KY, January/February 1996).

De Hart, J. S., "Second Wave Feminism(s) and the South: The Difference that Differences Make," in Farnham, C. A. (ed.), *Women of the American South* (New York: New York University Press, 1997).

Dobson, A., *Green Political Thought* (London: Routledge, 1990).

Dobson, J., *What Wives Wish Their Husbands Knew About Women* (Colorado Springs, CO: Focus on the Family and Tyndale, 1998).

Docherty, T. (ed.), *Postmodernism: A Reader* (Hemel Hempstead: Harvester Wheatsheaf, 1993).

Dominelli, L., *Women Across Continents: A Feminist Comparative Social Policy* (London: Harvester Wheatsheaf, 1991).

Eisenstein, Z., *The Radical Future of Liberal Feminism* (London: Longman, 1981).

Farnham, C. A. (ed.), *Women of the American South* (New York: New York University Press, 1997).

Foucault, M., *Madness and Civilization: A History of Insanity in the Age of Reason* (London: Tavistock, 1967).

Foucault, M., *The History of Sexuality Vol. 1* (Harmondsworth: Penguin, 1978).

Foucault, M., *The Order of Things* (London: Tavistock, 1970).

Fox-Genovese, E., *Within the Plantation Household: Black and White Women of the Old South* (Chapel Hill, NC: University Press, 1988).

Friedan, B., *The Feminine Mystique* (Harmondsworth: Penguin, 1965).

Friedman, J., *The Enclosed Garden: Women and Community in the Evangelical South 1830–1900* (Chapel Hill, NC: University Press, 1985).

Gilbert, S. and Gubar, S., *The Madwoman in the Attic: The woman writer and the nineteenth century* (New Haven, CN: Yale University Press, 1979).

Gilder, G., *Men and Marriage* (Gretna, LA: Pelican Publishers, 1986).

Goffman, E., *Stigma* (New York: Doubleday, 1968).

Goldberg, S., *The Inevitability of Patriarchy* (New York: William Morrow & Co., 1975).

Greer, G., *The Whole Woman* (London: Doubleday, 1999).

Hagler, H., *The Journal of Southern History* 46 (1980).

Hearn, J., *The Gender of Oppression* (New York: St. Martin's Press, 1987).

Herman, D., *Rights of Passage* (Toronto: Toronto University Press, 1994).

Hewitt, M., "Social policy and the question of postmodernism," *Social Policy Review* 6, 1994.

Humm, M. (ed.), *Feminisms* (London: Harvester Wheatsheaf, 1992).

Ivins, M., *Molly Ivins Can't Say That, Can She?* (New York: Vintage Books, 1992).

Jeffreys, S., *The Spinster and her Enemies: Feminism and Sexuality 1880–1930* (London: Pandora, 1985).

Jencks, C. (ed.), *The Post-Modern Reader* (London: Academy, 1993).

Kaplan, M., *Sexual Justice* (London: Routledge, 1997).

Kimmel, M. (ed.), *Changing Men* (London, Sage, 1987).

Kimmel, M. and Messner, M., *Men's Lives* 2nd edn (New York: Macmillan, 1992).

Kukathas, C. and Pettit, P., *Rawls: A Theory of Justice and its Critics* (Oxford: Polity Press, 1990).

Leland, J. and Miller, M., "Can Gays Convert?" *Newsweek* August 17, 1998.

Lockley, T., "A Struggle for Survival: Non-Elite White Women in Low-country Georgia, 1790–1830," in Farnham, C. A. (ed.), *Women of the American South* (New York: New York University Press, 1997).

Maxwell, J., "Driving Miss Norma," *World Magazine* (Asheville, N.C.: God's World Publications Inc., August 26/September 2 1995).

McCorvey, N. with Meisler, A., *I Am Roe: My Life, Roe v. Wade, and Freedom of Choice* (New York: HarperCollins, 1994).

Millett, K., *Sexual Politics* (London: Virago, 1977).

Minkowitz, D., "In the Name of the Father," *Ms. Magazine* (New York, November/December 1995), pp. 64–71.

Newman, D., *Then God Created Woman* (Colorado Springs, CO: Focus on the Family and Tyndale, 1998).

Okin, S. M., *Justice, Gender, and the Family* (New York: Basic Books, 1989).

Open Hands: Resources for Ministries Affirming the Diversity of Human Sexuality (Chicago, IL: Open Hands).

Operation Rescue, *Newsletter* September 25 1995.

Bibliography

Operation Rescue "Jesus is the Standard" (Dallas, TX: Operation Rescue, n.d.).

Pack, J. B., "Abortion: The Black Woman's Voice" (Jefferson City, MO: Easton Publishing Company, Inc., 1995).

Pateman, C., *The Sexual Contract* (Oxford: Polity Press, 1988).

Petchesky, R., *Abortion and Woman's Choice: The State, Sexuality and Reproductive Freedom* (London: Verso, 1986).

Phelan, S., *Getting Specific* (Minneapolis, MN: University of Minnesota Press, 1994).

Phillips, A., *Democracy & Difference* (University Park, Penn.: Pennsylvania State University Press, 1993).

Rawls, J., *A Theory of Justice* (Oxford: Oxford University Press, 1972).

Rich, A., *Of Woman Born: Motherhood as Experience and Institution* (London: Virago, 1977).

Roe *v.* Wade, 410 US 113 (1973).

Samar, V., *The Right to Privacy* (Philadelphia: Temple University Press, 1991).

Scanzoni, L. and Mollenkott, V. R., *Is the Homosexual My Neighbor?* (San Francisco, CA: Harpers & Row, 1980).

Sears, J., *Growing Up Gay in The South: Race, Gender and Journeys of the Spirit* (Binghamton, NY: Harrington Park Press, 1991).

Segrest, M. and Zeskind, L., *Quarantines and Death* (Atlanta, GA: Center for Democratic Renewal, 1989).

Silber, N., "The Northern Myth of the Rebel Girl," in Farnham, C. A. (ed.), *Women of the American South* (New York: New York University Press, 1997).

Smith, B., *Toward A Black Feminist Criticism* (Trumansburg, NY: The Crossing Press, 1980).

Trebilcot, J., *Dyke Ideas: Process, Politics, Daily Life* (New York: SUNY Press, 1994).

USA Today May 8 1996.

Ussher, J., *Women's Madness: Misogyny or Mental Illness* (London: Harvester Wheatsheaf, 1991).

Ussher, J. and Nicolson, P. (eds), *Gender Issues in Clinical Psychology* (London: Routledge, 1991).

Walby, S., *Theorizing Patriarchy* (Cambridge: Polity, 1990).

Weddington, S. *A Question of Choice* (New York: Penguin, 1992).

Weeks, J., "Rediscovering Values," in Squires, J. (ed.), *Principled Positions: Postmodernism and the Rediscovery of Value* (London: Lawrence and Wishart, 1993).

White, S. K., *Political Theory and Postmodernism* (Cambridge: Cambridge University Press, 1991).

Whites, L., "Stand by Your Man: The Ladies Memorial Association and the Reconstruction of Southern White Manhood," in Farnham, C. A. (ed.), *Women of the American South* (New York: New York University Press, 1997).

Wilkinson, R., *American Tough: The Tough Guy Tradition and American Character* (New York: Harper & Row, 1986).

Wilson, A., "Getting Your Kicks on Route 66: Stories of gay and lesbian life in rural America *c*. 1950–1970s," in Phillips, R., *et al.* (eds), *Non-Metropolitan Sexualities* (London: Routledge, 1999).

Young, I. M., *Justice and the Politics of Difference* (Princeton, NJ: Princeton University Press, 1990).

INDEX

Index

DATE DUE

The Library Store   #47-0106